LIVING...
THE TESTIMONY

WE CANNOT KEEP FROM SPEAKING ABOUT
WHAT WE HAVE SEEN AND HEARD.

—ACTS 4:20

Living ... The Testimony
Deidre D Havrelock

etcetera press LLC

Published by Etcetera Press LLC
Richland, WA
www.etcpress.net

ISBN: 978-1-936824-32-8
Library of Congress Control Number: 2013943862

Book series two:

LIVING...
THE TESTIMONY

DEIDRE D HAVRELOCK

ETCETERA PRESS
Richland, WA
2013

PERMISSIONS

FOR MY DAUGHTERS:
DEANNA, DARBY, AND DELANIE

SO MY TESTIMONY MIGHT BECOME PART
OF THEIR TESTIMONY.

WE WHO ARE DEDICATED TO HIM HONOR HIM NOT
ONLY WITH VOICE AND WORD, BUT ALSO WITH ALL
OF OUR SOUL, SO THAT WE VALUE TESTIMONY TO
HIM MORE THAN LIFE ITSELF.

—EUSEBIUS: THE CHURCH HISTORY

CONTENTS

Gratitude xiii

CHAPTER ONE
The Problem With Testimony 1

CHAPTER TWO
Why Am I So Dedicated to Testimony? 19

CHAPTER THREE
A Testimony is *Not* About God or Church 40

CHAPTER FOUR
A Testimony is *Not* About Faith 54

CHAPTER FIVE
A Testimony is *Not* About Us 65

CHAPTER SIX
What is a Strong Christian Testimony? 82

CHAPTER SEVEN
Generational Faith: *Passing on Your Testimony* 102

CHAPTER EIGHT
One Final Thought on Testimony: *Death* 118

Introduction to Book Three
Preparing ... The Testimony 126

Appendix
A Short Description of The Sabbath Rest:
Warning! It May Not Be What You Think! 128

Bibliography 141

About the Author 142

GRATITUDE

A big "Thank you!" goes out to those friends and family members who took the time to write their testimonies, allowing me to share them through this book. A special thank you goes out to my aunts, whose faith continues to inspire. Thank you to Ellen at Etcetera Press, for working so hard! And to my editor and fellow writer, Courtney Kasian, thank you for being wonderfully made and exceedingly helpful!

Book series two:

LIVING...
THE TESTIMONY

CHAPTER ONE

The Problem With Testimony

May I never boast of anything except the cross of our Lord
Jesus Christ, by which the world has been crucified to me, and
I to the world.

—Galatians 6:14

In 2005, my husband DJ and I, along with our three children,
moved to Saskatoon, Saskatchewan, Canada. It was here
I realized the Christian testimony was in great danger—
danger of becoming lukewarm and even irrelevant. What I
noticed was, somehow, over the years, our testimonies about
Jesus had worn away. No longer were testimonies about
Jesus: what he said/still says, what he taught/still teaches,
what he did/still does. Instead, when I heard Christians give
testimony (in churches, on T.V., and in books and magazines)
their stories consisted mostly of tragedy, sin, humble
beginnings, even human fortitude, along with a vague belief
in God. These testimonies were usually given without ever
mentioning Jesus in the process. Essentially, the testimony
of Jesus had become emotional and slightly mystical stories
primarily about us. I also noticed and began to purposefully

study that the stories most often viewed by Christians as "highly powerful" were those that made an audience cry and/ or dealt with relatable experiences, such as coping with or overcoming illness, death, work issues, and/or the finding of comfort and belonging. And although these stories were emotionally reassuring and even courageous, often citing a belief in God, I did suspect that a Christian testimony should somehow be primarily about Jesus.

Actually, my initial awareness over the difficulty we Christians have in presenting personal, clear, bold testimonies—specifically about Jesus—came through the pain and agony I endured during the writing of my own testimony. You see, soon after becoming a Christian I was inspired to write my testimony in the form of a book. The vision for this book came while I sat folding laundry. My testimony would be a memoir about my spiritual life, a story written for the average person. My testimony would be a true account about a young girl who was swallowed up by the occult, cried out to God, and was then led to Jesus—where she was miraculously healed. My testimony would inspire others to trust in Jesus.

Within a few years I had a first draft written. Soon after this, I sold the manuscript to a Christian publishing house. Once I moved to Saskatoon, I was on my final edit. Of course, having taken the initiative to write my testimony to such descriptive degrees, you might think I knew what I was doing. However, the opposite was true. I kept asking myself, "What is this 'testimony' ultimately about?" *My strange life?*

My family? My healing? The reality of the darkness? You see, I didn't understand what parts of my life to focus on, nor did I know what themes to structure the book around. Also, I was too intimidated to just be myself. Needless to say, after a few years of grappling with themes and structures—and shyness—I had a manuscript in my hands, but one with no clear purpose. My vision had become clouded.

Another part of my problem was I had sought out too much council and advice, without clearly sharing my own vision. Therefore, I had friends, leaders in the church, even a Christian publisher advising me that my testimony was for teenagers in the occult. With this advice ringing in my ears, my testimony slowly warped into a warning for Christians about the demonic and how evil and dangerous the occult can be. But the larger part of my problem was I didn't really understand what a Christian testimony was supposed to be about. In the end, when my publisher slotted my book to be released as a "fictional novel for Christians," I realized I needed to take a step back from publishing and refocus.

But honestly, even worse than writing my Christian testimony was speaking my testimony. This feat proved most difficult, especially after having written a manuscript. Whenever people asked me to share my personal faith, my mind suddenly filled with all sorts of details and emotions, climaxes and scene endings. I couldn't for the life of me tell my faith story concisely or quickly. During the absolute worst of cases, by the end of listening to my testimony, my captive audience was a mess of tears because of my tragedy. In these instances pity was the correlating response, followed by an, "I'm so sorry you had to go through all of that" remark. My mind would scream, "failure!" in these cases and rightly so. After all, I knew enough about the power of Jesus to know that a Christian testimony should offer, not only hope, but also, well ... victory.[1] Of course, I did experience a few glorious moments. I remember telling my story to a friend, and by the end she was in tears. She was in tears not because my life was so sad but because God was so good for sending Jesus to rescue me. This, I thought, is how a testimony should end. This is why the Bible's message is called "good news." But these moments seemed few and far between.

The scary part is, it took me literally years to realize what every testimony should be about: who Jesus is and what we have personally "seen and heard" in regard to who he is. Once I fully embraced this simple definition, I emailed my publisher expressing my anxiety over the direction my book was headed. My publisher was kind enough to let me out of my contract, so I could rework my manuscript as a non-fiction memoir. I now continue to write and edit my story, staying focused on its worth as a valuable spiritual journey—a personal memoir meant both for non-Christians and Christians alike, a journey that reflects not just my dark tragedy but also my true experience with Jesus.[2]

---

1. 1 Jn 5:4-5: "And this is the victory that conquers the world, our faith. Who is it that conquers the world but the one who believes that Jesus is the Son of God?"

2. My memoir is called *Saving Mary: The Possession and The Deliverance*. It is a spiritual memoir told in two books.

After realizing a personal testimony was supposed to be primarily about Jesus, I was forced to come against a huge assumption regarding Christian testimonies. As mentioned before, church leaders and friends had advised me that my testimony was for those who could relate to me. It wasn't for the average person. I was even told that I would never be able to share my personal testimony in a church because no one would be able to relate to the strange, dark events of my life—even though my troubled life culminated in a miraculous healing done in the name of Jesus. If this was true, then my rather dark testimony really was for people (most probably teenagers) struggling in the occult. I was told again and again that people wanted to hear about how to cope with life's everyday problems; my testimony didn't deliver.

However, by this time, through speaking my testimony I had helped a few members of my family and friends come to know Jesus—and none of them were struggling occult teenagers. Because of this, I began to fervently disagree with the notion that my faith story was only for certain people. I began to appreciate my story as one meant for the masses simply because listening to it gave people faith to believe in Jesus.

When giving our testimony we do not need to seek out a particular audience who may fit a certain criteria: people like us. We just need to tell people, any people, that Jesus is alive and he is the savior of humankind. Sometimes our personal story will connect with someone who has had a similar experience, but sometimes the truth of our story will connect with someone who simply needs to hear about the powerful reality of Jesus. Below is my testimony: the *how* along with the *why* I became a follower of Jesus. Notice that my story includes both what I initially *heard* about Jesus and what I *saw* faith in Jesus do. Finally, judge for yourself: is my strange story only for those struggling with the occult, or does it build your faith? *Does my testimony help you believe Jesus is God's Son, with power to heal?* Be warned, however. My story comes straight out of the Bible: demons, angels, Jesus—and all.

My Personal Testimony

I grew up in Edmonton, Alberta, Canada, as a Cree/Irish borderline Catholic girl, meaning this half-breed rarely went to Mass. However, I did pray every night. I absolutely loved God and believed in Him deeply. Being Catholic, I had heard about Jesus. In fact, my favorite song was "Away in a Manger." Whenever I was scared, which was often, I would sing this song. But I imagined Jesus to be a fairytale—a fantasy about a perfect God coming to save people. He was just for good thoughts. He was in no way a reality.

Despite my vague belief in Jesus, my relationship with God seemed deep. I would have conversations with my invisible God; I would tell God I loved Him. And I certainly did love Him. Although, I was becoming a bit frustrated with Him because of my dreary life circumstance. You see, my dad drank—a lot. And this stress, along with the stress of my quickly emerging spiritual life, was simply too overwhelming.

The Problem With Testimony

As a child I lived with a strange secret. I sensed an ominous yet deeply intriguing spiritual force in my home. I simply assumed a ghost lived in my house. To convolute matters even more, when I was just seven, a man with fire for hair appeared to me in a dream, forcing me to marry him in front of an upside-down cross. He told me in the dream, "Don't worry, you have been chosen." From this point on, I completely believed I was married to the devil—irrevocably dark and aligned with evil.

Fortunately, this dream did motivate me to dig my heels in and search for God. I figured only God could get me divorced from the devil. But instead my search led me to Fred, a kind spirit I met in grade four through a Ouija board. Being Cree, spirits were nothing new to me. My mom's family always talked about spirits. Most of my aunts and uncles were scared of the spirits or ghosts they saw in their dreams and in their houses, but my grandmother told me the spirits were there to help and protect us. I wasn't quite sure what to believe. I was confused. After all, the spirits I sensed around me and the ones I saw in my dreams scared me, too. But then again, Fred seemed different. This spirit was nice. He was funny. Fred told me through the Ouija board that his job was to protect and watch over me. Eventually, I began telling myself that spirits just felt creepy, but once you got to know them they could be nice. Especially, if you were nice to them.

Fred became my constant companion. But one day, in grade six, after my best friend's dad tried to molest me and just after my uncle Glen (who had sexually molested me as a small child) came to live with us in our home, I had a nervous breakdown. While left home alone with Glen, I grabbed a butcher knife and ran to my room to hide. Once in my bedroom, instead of picking up my Ouija board to call on Fred, I cried out to God, telling Him I wanted to kill myself. Suddenly I heard a voice speak out loud: "When you are big everything will be okay." It was God; He spoke to me. He was real.[3] I told God I'd hang on until I was *big,* which obviously, to a twelve-year-old mind, meant eighteen.

By age sixteen, things seemed to have miraculously changed for the better. First of all, my dad was now inexplicably healed from alcoholism. Second, I was introduced by my high school teacher to a New Age transcendental meditation and channeling group that met weekly in the back room of a small bookstore.[4] I was so excited. I thought for sure—in this extremely spiritual group—I would find God and get my divorce from Satan.

This group also told me spirits were good and helpful. However, a few sessions later, I found myself strangely altered after my spirit guide Fred, along with another extremely violent spirit, entered my body during group meditation and refused to leave. A member of the group did attempt to help me force these spirits from my body, but the endeavor failed. Consequently, I was kicked out of my New Age group for

---

3. God spoke to me long before I became a Christian, so non-Christians can hear the voice of God, too. It is obvious to me now that God was with me through my whole ordeal, working to reveal Christ to me.

4. Channeling is when you place yourself in a relaxed and open state in order to allow a spirit to enter your body and speak directly through you.

having *bad karma*. This meant *I* was the one attracting these evil spirits to the group—because I was evil. I left the group feeling deeply hurt, misunderstood, and very aware of being "chosen" by the devil.[5]

A school friend of mine named Doug, who had joined the channeling group with me, then suggested, without knowing anything about my spiritual past, that I study Satanism. His brother had a Satanic Bible.[6] After flatly declining, I began dreaming I was killing people. I also dreamed of horrible evil creatures. Rats invading my house was a common dream, and the devil with fire for hair began reappearing in my dreams, growing angrier every time I refused to follow him. When I turned eighteen, I gave up on spirituality. I simply wouldn't choose Satan and God had failed to show up and save me.

When I was twenty-two years old, now bulimic/ anorexic, depressed, and suffering from intense back pain, my life took an unexpected turn when at work God surprisingly spoke to me again saying, "This is the man whom you shall marry." That man was DJ, a young man who worked in the same office as I did. Eventually DJ and I began dating, and even though we seemed to have nothing in common— because I was convinced that God had sent him to help me— on our third date, I opened up to him, describing to him my nightmares and my spirit guide, Fred. Of course, I worried DJ might consider me crazy, but instead he said, "I'm here to

---

5. These experiences are described in book one of my spiritual memoir, *Saving Mary: The Possession*.

6. Doug later became a Christian, after two Christians took the time to speak to him about Jesus. I got to know Doug again through *Facebook*.

help."[7]

It was a few weeks later that DJ opened up to me, explaining how he believed in Jesus. He told me he believed Jesus was alive. He told me Jesus could heal me and save me; and because he was God's actual Son, he was the gateway to knowing and experiencing God. DJ asked me to simply *trust Jesus*.[8]

But I was more than a little doubtful. In fact, his Christian beliefs made me furious. It seemed idiotic for anyone to believe that a childhood fairytale could be true, and it seemed positively arrogant that DJ thought he knew and understood God. After all, why couldn't God just save me Himself? *What did He need Jesus for? Why was Jesus so important?* I argued with DJ about the relevance of Jesus many times. Then one night, after arguing about Jesus yet again, my back flared up with pain. DJ asked if he could pray for me. I was uncomfortable with this but thought, *What will it hurt?*

As DJ prayed for me, particularly when he asked me to be healed "in the name of Jesus," my back pain sharply escalated—then the voices began. It was just like during my channeling days. Spirits stirred inside me wanting to speak. Except this time they were enraged. As DJ continued praying, my body contorted as my muscles tightened; a low growl came from my lips. Within seconds, a thick black mass pulled out from my back and hovered above us. I remember

---

7. DJ later confided in me, telling me he had heard the Holy Spirit speak to him as an inner whisper, saying, "This is why you are here (to help this girl)." DJ's testimony is shared in Chapter Five.

8. These events are described in book two, *Saving Mary: The Deliverance*.

huddling against DJ, whispering, "What is that?"

"It's evil," he said.

I was terrified. DJ, however, immediately told the evil spirits to "leave, in the name of Jesus." Surprisingly, the blackness retreated back down inside me. I was horrified and confused, crying and shaking. I didn't understand I was possessed. All I knew was that Fred and another spirit were living inside me; they were angry, extremely strong, and they absolutely hated the name Jesus.

DJ, now with clear confirmation that my problem was actually demonic possession, had to find help, but where was he to go? He wasn't sure if his church leadership would believe him. DJ then met with a Christian girl, Audrey, who also worked in our office.[9] She and DJ decided to bring me to her church. They hoped her pastor could pray for me and expel the evil spirits.[10]

DJ convinced me to attend a service. However, shortly after arriving at the church, I found myself running from the service after voices in my head told me to kill the pastor. I remember this pastor was preaching about Jesus being able to heal. The whole service felt strange and uncomfortable to me, but DJ convinced me to go back to this church two more times. Each time I returned, the strength and rage of the voices grew and my strange back pain returned. Finally, much too terrorized and confused to go on, I refused to go

---

9. I contacted Audrey and asked her to go through this story before it went to print. As you can imagine, I am greatly thankful to Audrey for helping me. We were all in our twenties back then.

10. I knew nothing about these plans.

back. I told DJ talking about Jesus aggravated my problems, so the solution was obviously *not* to talk about him.

DJ and Audrey began to pray that I would change my mind about returning to the church. They were desperate for me to change my mind because they had arranged for me to meet with a man who happened to be teaching about the spiritual realm at Audrey's church that week. They were hoping this visiting Christian preacher would be able to carry out my deliverance. But they weren't sure how to get me to my appointment, which they had already scheduled.

The night before my appointment I had a dream. A brilliant light appeared shouting the word "Jericho" at me. The next morning, I told DJ that I saw an angel and that the angel had given me a message—that message was simply the word "Jericho."[11] DJ explained to me that the word "Jericho" was actually a city named in the Bible: God destroys the city of Jericho, but saves a trusting woman through Joshua, the leader of God's army. The words in the story that impacted me most were: "But the Lord said to Joshua, 'Jericho and its king and all its mighty warriors are already defeated, for I have given them to you!'" (Josh 6:2, TLB[12]). I suddenly was sure of one thing: I knew God was telling me not to fear the angry and seemingly strong spirits inside me because *somehow* He had already defeated them. All I needed to do was get myself inside the church and trust God to do it; God had finally come to save me.

---

11. Reminiscent of Heb 1:14: "Are not all angels spirits in the divine service, sent to serve for the sake of those who are to inherit salvation?"

12. The Bible version we were reading at this time was The Living Bible.

So now, one last time, I headed for the church. As I entered the church, the voices returned, my back flared up with intense pain, and I began drifting in and out of consciousness. After managing to make my way upstairs where my "exorcist" waited for me, I lost complete consciousness just as I entered the room. The last thing I remember was seeing a rather short man standing in the room and hearing the words, "Everybody get out!" come from my mouth. I also remember worrying that if DJ and Audrey left me, the evil spirits inside me might actually kill this preacher.

I regained consciousness on the opposite side of the room as the preacher said to me, "Deidre, it's time to choose. You must choose now." At first, I didn't understand what he meant. *Why did I have to choose? Who was I supposed to choose?* All my life, wasn't I choosing God? And yet choosing God wasn't working. In all truth, I just wanted God to step in and save me; I wanted Him to put an end to this whole nightmare. I didn't want to have to choose anyone. But then I remembered: God had sent DJ to help me and DJ had told me to trust Jesus. There and then I decided to do it. I would trust Jesus. I responded, "Jesus." Just the one word. Immediately the spirits flew out of my body and a different, gentle Spirit came in.[13] I knew this new spiritual presence was God. I began crying as God wrapped around me like a hug. I remember thinking,

---

13. I called my spiritual memoir *Saving Mary: The Possession and The Deliverance* because Mary Magdalene was the woman from whom Jesus cast out seven demons; see Mk 16:9. I, however, only had two demons.

"I've finally made it home. God has come for me."[14]

I left the church that night thinking how I would never speak about this event again. I even told DJ we would keep it a secret. I understood that because I had aligned myself with and sought the help of Jesus that I was now a Christian, but I really had no understanding as to what this meant. Actually, the whole thing frightened me quite a bit. *What did it mean to be a Christian? Would people now hate me or treat me differently because of my choice? Would I have to go to church?* I knew Jesus had saved me and that he had even healed me (I was no longer bulimic or anorexic after this event and my back pain disappeared[15]), and I was quite thankful and awed by all of this. But in reality, I simply wanted to leave my past behind and go on with a normal life. I wasn't sure how or even *if* Jesus would be part of this new life.

With the demonic now behind us, DJ and I were left to fall in love and dream about getting married. Unfortunately, this wasn't possible. This wasn't possible because I wasn't able to fully trust in marriage. I still had the idea of being married to Satan in my mind; therefore, marriage felt extremely dark and oppressive to me. I began imagining DJ morphing into an overbearing, evil husband. Strangely enough, I began pushing DJ to marry me. At the time, I figured if DJ and I married

---

14. I also began speaking in "tongues," even though I had no idea what tongues was. You can imagine how confused I was! Confused, yet exceedingly happy.

15. I don't mean to suggest that the demons caused me to be bulimic. I chose to be bulimic to counteract my binge eating. Binge eating was my actual problem. The binge eating was horrific. After my deliverance the drive to binge eat was gone, and I quit being bulimic. The demons definitely seemed to be the cause of my back pain.

quickly then the intense feeling of fear that I was beginning to experience would go away. But as soon as DJ and I got engaged, my fear intensified—and so I ran. I hopped on a plane headed for California, thinking it would be better for the both of us if I were to remain single. However, I really did love DJ; so two days later, an incredibly troubled girl returned home praying, "Please God, help me not to be afraid of marriage." I even began carrying around a sticky note in my purse that read, "My husband is faithful and kind; I like being married." Whenever I got nervous, which was often, I would read this positive affirmation.[16]

DJ and I were married on September 10th, 1994.

I had set out as a child to find God and obtain a divorce from Satan. I desperately wanted to know that the spiritual bond the devil had created with me through marriage could be wiped out forever. The night of my wedding I had another dream. A man dressed all in white, glowing from head to foot, handed me a brilliant white telegram stamped with a royal seal. The telegram read, "Congratulations on Marrying a King! Welcome to the Family of God. Your Inheritance is Located at …"

My inheritance turned out to be a house—a mansion that looked to be made of gold. I awoke from this dream completely aware I was no longer married to the devil but married instead to God's Son, Jesus—King of Heaven. My

---

16. I had previously taken a self-help course through work where they taught that positive affirmation notes could help us deal with uncomfortable circumstances. At first I thought this was a dumb idea, but I used that note a lot!

divorce had finally come. After telling DJ this dream, he pulled out his Bible and he pointed out the following verse to me:

> Let not your heart be troubled [says Jesus]. You are trusting God, now trust in me. There are many homes up there where my Father lives, and I am going to prepare them for your coming. —*Jn 14:1-3, TLB*

It was after this dream that I knew my heart would always belong to Jesus. No longer would I think of him as just a fairy tale, or merely a powerful person who simply rushes in to save the day. I now thought of him as the Son of God *and …* my friend. After all, he had spoken to me personally. Jesus told me, "Don't let your heart be troubled. I know you trust God. Now trust in me."

৵ ৶

I tell you my story so you may see a basic truth: even the simplest testimony about Jesus—such as the one DJ told me—can destroy the best-laid plans of Satan. Incidentally, the testimony DJ gave to me had very little to do with his own life story, but everything to do with who Jesus is: "Jesus is alive. Jesus can heal and save. He is God's actual Son. He is the gateway to knowing and experiencing God. *Trust Jesus.*"

One of my most memorable experiences with sharing my rather strange personal testimony happened when I emailed my story to a science journalist who was looking for personal accounts regarding women and dreams. He wanted to know how women were affected by their dreams and if dreams helped with life's issues. After receiving my email, he called me up for an interview, asking me numerous questions about my life experience and about other dreams I had. By the end of our rather long conversation, he said he wasn't sure if he would be able to use my story in his upcoming article, but he was glad I had taken the time to share my experience with him. Since as a science guy, he never knew such amazing spiritual things, such as Jesus casting out demons, took place. I was overwhelmed with gratitude to God after this. After all, I had shared my experience of Jesus with a complete stranger—one with whom I had nothing in common—and, surprisingly, he had said, "Thank you."

The truth is, we are not called and anointed to tell interesting stories of family tragedy, humble beginnings, or human fortitude. We are here to reveal the truth about Jesus. If our testimonies do slowly turn away from being about Jesus, focusing more (or wholly) upon ourselves and/or our worldly experiences (such as incest, rape, suicide, murder, greed, occult activities, divorce, illness, motherhood, fatherhood, or even business), then they are no longer testimonies. They have become personal ministries. For example, I sometimes speak about the dangers of the demonic and the occult, but my ministering to people (giving them sound advice, listening to their experiences, and helping them cope with and overcome certain issues, of which I have experience) though fabulous, is not what testimony is about. We minister to people, but we testify about Jesus. Often times, we learn to do both simultaneously.

This book is about giving Jesus more than average thought. *Who is Jesus? How do I know who Jesus is? What aspect of Jesus has been revealed to me, personally? And am I fully prepared and happily willing to testify about my faith in Jesus through both my deeds and words? Or, am I afraid and / or unprepared to live out and speak about my faith—often testifying about other things instead?*

The early disciples and apostles in the Bible always testified about who Jesus is and what he had done or taught. However, in our day and age we are experiencing a growing cultural trend of testifying about: *ourselves, God / church,* or sometimes we speak about *faith* in general terms. Our lack of clarity—when we specifically want or are asked to give our Christian testimony—is causing our testimonies to become weak and even irrelevant.

* For a review of this chapter and to answer reflective questions, see the companion guide: *Preparing ... The Testimony.*

CHAPTER TWO

Why Am I So Dedicated to Testimony?

But they have conquered him [Satan] by the blood of the Lamb
and by the word of their testimony.

—Revelation 12:11

My favorite show used to be *Stargate SG-1*. I enjoyed this
show for the obvious reasons: alien shoot-outs, bumbling
yet brilliant characters, and of course, well ... space. (I'm
crazy for any show that starts, "Somewhere in a distant
galaxy ... ") But I also liked this show for the less obvious
reasons: insightful perspectives on religion.

Take for instance Stargate's second movie, *The Ark of Truth*.
A quick synopsis goes like this: powerful, almost miraculous,
aliens called the Ori use the guise of "We are Gods, worship
us—or die" to enslave various alien worlds, all while rebel
aliens (including Humans and the far more advanced race of
Alterans) attempt to fight back. As the Humans (Stargate's
SG-1 team) zip around the galaxy blowing up Ori ships (while
trying in vain to convince others that the Ori are *not* gods),

the Alterans let slip that (millions of years earlier) they had built an Ori destruction machine called the "Ark of Truth." One look into this powerful ark forced its curious viewers to believe this truth: *The Ori are lying and are not gods. They are power-hungry aliens—do not worship them!*

The Alterans, however, found a problem with their machine. Their dilemma, of course, was forced indoctrination. If the Alterans used their machine, would they not be the same as the Ori, literally forcing their views on others? In the end, the Alterans rejected their own indoctrination machine and instead buried it, agreeing that "the only moral way to change someone's mind—make them see the truth—is to present evidence."

A Christian testimony, like all testimonies, is about presenting evidence in order to back up a claim that is purported to be true. Hebrews 11:1-2 tells us, "Now faith is the substance of things hoped for, the evidence of things not seen. For by it the elders obtained a good testimony" (NKJV). Simply put, an active kind of faith produces substance. And it is this substance that works as our evidence. In other words, our hope is in Jesus being the actual Son of God, with power to help and heal, *and* teach with perfect wisdom about spiritual things. This hope in who Jesus is will eventually produce evidence (substance) in our lives, and it is this evidence (our changed beliefs, changed character, changed desires, acts of service, physical healings, spiritual encounters, and spiritual understanding) that is to be offered up as part of our testimony. Our goal then, in testifying about Jesus, is not to provide the world with undeniable proof (beyond a shadow of a doubt) that Jesus is the world's Messiah. But rather, our mission is to boldly offer a genuine account of our spiritual beliefs and experiences, that when combined with other testimonies,[17] provides "reasonable evidence" to believe Jesus is alive and is the world's hope. It is the Christian testimony, our experiences and beliefs as followers of a living Jesus, that brings to light, explains, authenticates, and confirms— not only the message of the Bible, but also the events of the Bible—revealing to the world Jesus' true nature, his purpose, his unending existence, and God's loving character and plan. Together, through testifying, we reveal the reality of Jesus.

Granted, providing people with personal testimony takes both patience and time, more time than a super powerful indoctrination machine would require (which, by the way, the SG-1 team digs up and actually uses, thereby saving the galaxy). Despite this, taking time to testify really is the moral way to go about bringing people to truth.

How Did I Begin Giving Testimony?

My own deep interest with testimony initially began about a year after I became a Christian. Actually, it began with a wildly strange dream.[18] I was newly married and living on an acreage with my husband when I dreamed Jesus was returning

---

17. Remember in *Studying ... The Testimony,* how God required two or three testimonies to be given in court. People often need to hear more than one testimony in order to confirm truth.

18. God has often spoken to me through dreams; reminiscent of Job 33:14-15.

to earth. In my dream, I was about to commit adultery with a complete stranger when suddenly I heard something. I'm not sure what the sound was; but upon hearing it, I instantly knew Jesus was returning. I was completely shocked. I was also mortified regarding my preceding intentions. There I stood—thunderstruck and guilty. But then overwhelming joy filled me. I began exclaiming, "Jesus is coming!" I ran out of my house and down a highway, shouting what I knew was good news: "Jesus is coming! Jesus is coming!"

All around me huge meteors plunged from the sky, slamming into cars and houses. The world was in complete chaos, but I wasn't scared. I was simply too thrilled. I kept shouting, "Jesus is coming!" Then I stopped. Before me, up in the sky, I saw a planet. Somehow the sky had changed. Instead of seeing the sun, a huge planet now loomed on the horizon. It was an awesome sight. Shocked, I blurted, "The earth has shifted its axis!" Then I continued with my exciting news, "Jesus is coming!"[19]

At this point, I decided to run and tell my mom the good news. I opened her front door, saw her standing in her kitchen with her back toward me, and I vibrantly declared, "Mom, Jesus is coming!"

Slowly she turned; she looked me straight in the eye and said, "Who?"

---

19. I had this dream before I read the Bible—a dream about Mt 24:29, 44: "The sun will be darkened, and the moon will not give its light; the stars will fall from heaven, and the powers of heaven will be shaken. ... Therefore you also must be ready, for the Son of Man is coming at an unexpected hour."

I awoke from this dream completely dazed. What stunned me most was not that I was about to commit adultery just as Jesus was returning to earth or that I had witnessed the earth shift its axis, thrusting the whole world into some kind of crazy end-time mode, but that my mom didn't know who Jesus was. No one had ever explained him or his purpose to her—certainly not me. In fact, at this point in my Christian life, I had no intention of ever telling anyone about Jesus.

You see, I had decided after becoming a Christian that I would keep my experience with Jesus and the decision I made about following him safely stored away in the back of my mind, with the blinds pulled down and the lights metaphorically flicked off. I decided I would treasure Jesus and the words he personally spoke to me in my heart, but I certainly would not share him with others. I just felt my spiritual life story along with my experience of Jesus was simply too strange. Therefore, it was much too embarrassing to talk about.

This dream about Jesus and my mom obviously changed things for me. I realized that completely forgetting about what Jesus had done for me was not an option—or I just might lose my way in life. I also became desperate to introduce my mom to Jesus. After all, I didn't want her to completely miss out on someone so wonderful. In all truth, I felt awful. If Jesus was coming back—at any moment—shouldn't I be waiting with eager expectation? In fact, shouldn't everyone have the opportunity to wait with the thrill of expectancy? Especially my mom? *But how would I tell her? What would I say?*

I decided to read the Bible to figure out what to do. Because my dream was about the return of Jesus, I started my journey into the Bible with the book of Revelation. I simply started with the end, and I soon came upon Revelation 12:10-11:

> Then I heard a loud voice in heaven, proclaiming, "Now have come the salvation and the power and the kingdom of our God and the authority of his Messiah, for the accuser of our comrades has been thrown down, who accuses them day and night before our God. But they have conquered him by the blood of the Lamb and by the word of their testimony, for they did not cling to life even in the face of death."
> —*Rev 12:10-11*

I realized through this verse that my "testimony" (which, at the time, I assumed was the story of *how* I became a Christian) held great power: power to defeat our accuser—Satan.[20] This hit me as incredibly appealing. After all, I had spent my childhood being tormented by Satan. Now it was like God was telling me He wanted me to fight back and conquer, simply by sharing what I knew about Jesus. I became immediately willing.

Because an angel had once appeared to me in a dream shouting the word "Jericho," the next thing I decided to

---

20. Satan condemns the world; Christ redeems it. See Jn 3:17: "Indeed, God did not send the Son into the world to condemn the world, but in order that the world might be saved through him."

do was reread this story.[21] I was thinking, maybe there was something in this story that I missed during my first, rather brief, reading. Something that might shed light on how, exactly, I was to go about giving testimony. And there was.

On my second reading, I saw Joshua as a metaphor for Jesus[22]coming to save, not only me, but also Rahab's *whole* family. After all, as the story goes, Rahab said to the Israelite men who had been sent to spy out Jericho:

> The LORD your God is indeed God in heaven above and on earth below. Now then, since I have dealt kindly with you, swear to me by the LORD that you in turn will deal kindly with my family. Give me a sign of good faith that you will spare my father and mother, my brothers and sisters, and all who belong to them, and deliver our lives from death. —*Josh 2:11-13*

The spies agreed to spare Rahab and her family *if* Rahab could convince her family to stand with her—in her house. Rahab's house became their salvation.[23] I then deduced that Rahab must have gone to her family, telling them what she knew about the coming of Joshua. Surprisingly, they must have believed her. After all, by the time Joshua came, Rahab's

---

21. The story of Joshua, Rahab, and the city of Jericho is found in Joshua 2. Joshua is sent to overtake the city, sending two spies ahead of himself. Rahab is the woman who pleads with the spies on behalf of her whole family.

22. "Joshua" is the name "Jesus" in Hebrew; it means "Jehovah-saved." Jesus means "Jehovah-saved" in Greek.

23. Reminiscent of the scripture, Josh 24:15: "As for me and my household, we will serve the LORD." Also reminiscent of Wisdom's house in Prov 9:1-4.

family was safe in her house.[24] So, for myself, wanting my own family to come to know Jesus, I decided I would go to them and tell them what I knew about him. But before I did that, I prayed, asking God to deal kindly with my family and to please, "Bring us all home. With no one left out." I then began to meet with family members. My aunt G— was first.[25] Since this aunt (my dad's sister) had already told me she was a Christian, I figured this would be a safe place to practice telling my "faith story."

Unfortunately, my aunt's reaction was not what I expected. She was taken aback by my revealing to her that I had not only accepted the reality of Jesus, but that Jesus had cast out demons from me. Her skepticism devastated me. It wasn't that she didn't believe in the existence of demons; rather, she found it hard to believe that I had been demonized—me, her fun-loving niece, whom she knew very well, and whom she had even taken to church on numerous occasions. Well, thankfully, my aunt chose to believe me and my story. In the end, my testimony validated the reality of the Bible for her. We soon became prayer partners with a mission—to pray for and give testimony to others.[26]

I then told my testimony to my girlfriend. After that, I told it to another aunt of mine. After this, Aunt G— and I

---

24. See Josh 6:23.

25. I have decided to keep this name confidential.

26. It was around this time that I received the vision of writing my testimony out as a book.

began to pray for and meet with my elder brother, Gilbert.[27] During the process of praying for my brother, my aunt's atheist husband, to my surprise, became a Christian. My aunt and I then spoke with my dad. Below is my dad's testimony that he recently wrote out for me. By reading my dad's testimony you can better understand my own personal testimony, *and* you can see how God is so willing to work through entire families. This process of healing a family, however, does often take years.

Dad's Testimony

> "God grant me the serenity to accept the things I cannot change, courage to change the things I can, and the wisdom to know the difference."
> —*Serenity Prayer by Reinhold Niebuhr*

I muttered these twenty-six supposedly life-changing words meeting after meeting, year after year, from before I was old enough to enter a bar and for the sixteen years following. The first time I heard these words was with my father, an alcoholic, who after getting me out of a two-year jail sentence, thought we should both take a look at our drinking. But the drinking continued; and consequently, so did the meetings.

As the years went by, I drank. I attended A.A. meetings and rehab centers; I also prayed to God and I listened to the old-timers who told me three things: do the twelve steps, ask

---

27. My brother eventually became a believer of Christ. He described his moment with Jesus to me one day during a summer visit. He passed away on October 27th, 2010.

God to remove all your shortcomings, and follow what the Alcoholics Anonymous big book says. I did these things and I believed they could get me sober.

In my heart I wanted so to be a good father, to be a good husband. But the greater I failed, the more desperate my drinking became; the more desperate my drinking became, the greater I failed. I was not working my A.A. program out very well. I couldn't "Let go and let God." "Welcome back" became my mantra. And then I had what I thought at first was a dream.

One night as I was lying on the couch asleep, hung over and depressed, a dark figure appeared and stood watching me from the foot of the couch. It was tall, thin, and seemingly faceless. The horrid, malicious feeling of its presence terrified me, and I screamed with pure fear. It was at this time that I understood completely and irrevocably that evil existed *and* ... I was living with it.

"Courage is being scared to death but saddling up anyway." *—John Wayne*

"God grant me the courage ... " I could find no courage in myself and though I tried, I could not find courage through A.A. Ultimately, after this "dream" I simply could not find courage to face myself or what I had become. I definitely could not saddle up. On New Year's Day, 1983, I returned to an empty house, my family once again gone. I knew it was for good this time. Now I began to drink, to live my life with a definite goal—total self-destruction.

Growing up I sometimes went to church, to Bible summer camps; I even went to a Christian college the last two years of high school, after being sent there as punishment for my behavior. However, it was at my grandmother's house where I actually listened about Jesus. She seemed to be the only person who didn't condemn me as she told me that Jesus saves. I remember her telling me about how she prayed for Jesus to heal her from psoriasis, and miraculously, one night, the dried scabs that covered her body all fell off. Unfortunately, my understanding about Jesus was cut short by my grandmother's death. I did know, however, that I should be turning to Jesus for help and answers—that much had gotten through to me. But two problems existed. First, I knew with Jesus you had to turn your whole life over to him—all the parts, not just the ones you wanted changed. I also knew that if I did choose Jesus I would quit drinking, and that was terrifying. *How do you deal with everything you've done wrong once you're sober?*

Alcoholics Anonymous did not acknowledge Jesus. They, in fact, discouraged me from turning to Jesus by telling me I could choose anything to act as my higher power. In reality, they simply wanted us to understand there was help other than ourselves out there. I, however, believed that Jesus needed to be in on this strengthening of my heart, but I had absolutely no conviction as to my approach. I also doubted very much that prayer actually worked for the "greatly sinful" individual like myself. After all, I had no proof in my own life. The A.A. meetings continually reinforced the promise that believing in a generic higher power would fill the expanding void inside me.

The night of November 30, 1983, while living in a skid row hotel, I finally called out to Jesus for help. With heart and soul, I screamed out. Not to save me, nor to give me, but to take me, to let me die and take me.

December 1ˢᵗ, I awoke.

Pain engulfed me as I remembered a night call to my thirteen-year-old daughter, Deidre. I had wanted to say goodbye; she hung up crying.[28] Here I was still alive—Jesus hadn't answered my prayer. "Thanks a lot," I muttered. I got up and headed downstairs. *The bar should be open, time to start all over again.*

The beer arrives to my table and it sits. I don't understand. I've been on a nine-month binge; my whole body is shaking, traumatized from the overnight lack of alcohol. That beer sitting in front of me is the cure, and yet, oddly, I don't want it. I get up and I walk outside into the sunlight. The first thing I notice is that it is now winter; my thin fall jacket is useless. I walk down the avenue shivering and wondering. I know with all my being that something is different. The light feels good and my desire to crawl into the darkness is gone.

In 1999 I joined the Christian Motorcyclist Association. It was at this time that I surrendered to God and fully accepted Jesus as my savior. This total commitment, after all, seemed the sensible thing to finally do. And anyone who

---

28. I remember the call, and I describe the event in my spiritual memoir, *Saving Mary: The Possession*. My brother and I prayed that God would save our dad that night.

knows me knows that I am very seldom sensible. My short-term memory is poor, as are my pockets. However, these are the facts, and I tell you they are true.

Evil exists.

The Holy Spirit is the source of all truth.

Jesus is the answer.

I am a sinner.

My sins are forgiven.

My desire to drink was completely extinguished on December 1st, 1983, and I remain in the sunlight and out of the dark, even when it's cloudy.[29]

æ ❧

After telling my dad about my own encounter with Jesus, I then went to my aunt Myrna. Here I sensed something. As I told her my testimony, she listened with uncomfortable interest. I left her house not knowing if something good had happened or something drastically bad. I began eagerly praying for her.

A year later, Myrna phoned. I asked her to travel the four hours to my house to visit me. During our visit, Myrna asked me to again tell her my story. Which, I did. I then told her more about what I knew about Jesus. As I spoke with her, suddenly a verse from John 14 popped into my head: "They who have my commandments and keep them are those

---

29. My dad was able to write out his testimony for me after he read an early draft of this book. Before that I had never known the complete story.

who love me; and those who love me will be loved by my Father, and I will love them and reveal myself to them" (Jn 14:21). Before I knew it, I was telling Myrna the hardest part of becoming a Christian was that first step—believing in Jesus. "But after that," I explained, "Jesus will come and he will reveal himself to you, and you will know he is alive." I couldn't believe what I was saying. *Was I promising Myrna that Jesus would in fact reveal himself to her?* I was wishing I could yank those words back. Thank goodness I couldn't. Below is Myrna's testimony:

Aunt Myrna's Testimony

A few years ago I lost a job that was incredibly satisfying to me. Unfortunately, my husband and I were now not only broke, but also heavily in debt—quickly sinking into financial destitution. (Tim Hortons wouldn't even hire me and the food bank was becoming a very real option to us!) It was during this time that Deidre first told me about her experiences with Jesus. Afterwards, other people kept coming to me with their "God stories." My first thought was, "Is there an X on my forehead?" The next time Deidre asked me to come down to visit, I asked her to tell me her story again. This time at the end of our conversation she told me, "Myrna, the hardest, most necessary part toward restoring our relationship with God is taking that first step, placing our hope fully in Jesus. After this type of commitment is made, Jesus will reveal himself and you will know he has risen and is alive." And it stuck. I made the commitment in my heart.

I drove home with a book Deidre gave me about prayer. I decided to pray; I sat at my kitchen table with an old Bible I found in the house and said, "Dear God, I've tried to read your Bible before and it didn't make sense to me. Will you please give me something just for me?!" I opened the Bible, placing my finger on what I thought was just any passage and it read:

> To the angel of the church at **Smyrna** write: "These are the words of the First and the Last, who was dead and came to life again: I know how hard pressed and poor you are, but in reality you are rich."[30]

༪ ༕

Within the year, my aunt Myrna gathered together a group of her closest friends, and in a meeting room at Chapters bookstore I met with them, telling them all my testimony. One of Myrna's friends became a disciple of Jesus after that meeting. About a year later, Myrna's husband became a Christian.

Myrna then said she wanted to pray for my uncle Glen.[31] We also began praying, during this same time, for my aunt Jackie who was angry and bitter toward our family. Consequently, she had estranged herself from us ten years prior. Myrna and I, before we could deliver testimony to

---

30. From Rev 2:8-9 (REB), bold added.

31. Glen's story can be found in the first book of this series, *Studying … The Testimony*. Glen died shortly after becoming a Christian.

Jackie, because she was estranged, first had to ask God to bring her back into the family. Jackie came back to the family due to Glen's death; she attended his funeral. The moment she walked into the church basement, where Glen's wake was held, I knew God had plans to bring her home—and to Jesus. Her appearance made Glen's funeral rather joyful. After Jackie came back, both Myrna and I gave Jackie our testimonies. However, it took two years for Jackie's hard, angry heart to break down, but eventually it did break. It was a few months after she attempted suicide by overdose that she made the decision to become a disciple of Jesus.

After becoming a Christian in November of 2004, joining a church, and being baptized, Jackie then began praying for her lawyer. You see, after she had tried to commit suicide her husband left her; he now wanted complete custody of their three children. Below is part of Jackie's testimony. Notice through this story that even though Jackie was a brand new Christian, with her feet just barely wet, her joy in a living Jesus simply could not be contained, even though her life was in a shambles.

Aunt Jackie's Testimony

A season in my life hit hard. Little did I know, four years ago, that I would be traveling on an unbelievable journey of faith. Trials (court room trials, that is) and tribulations assailed me one after another, seeming never to relent. My life and the lives of my three young sons changed dramatically as I entered into a bitter custody battle with my husband.

During the custody trials my first lawyer quit, referring me to a second counselor. This lawyer, unbeknownst to me, began to pilfer funds from my account. Once I realized what was happening, I found the courage, strength, and perseverance through the Bible to represent myself in a second courtroom drama against my now ex-legal representative.

As a Christian, Jesus carried me during this nine-month ordeal. I felt as though he was wiping my tears as I cried at work and at home—at night my pillow was completely wet with missing my three young sons and not knowing how I was ever going to get through.

A year later, after successfully getting my money back and after reading, "love your enemies" in the Bible, I decided to pray for my ex-lawyer as I read the book of Luke and saw that there were "experts in law" in Jesus' time. In Luke 11:46 (NIV) Jesus says, "And you experts in the law, woe to you, because you load people down with burdens they can hardly carry, and you yourselves will not lift one finger to help them." I prayed for my ex-lawyer's name to be written in Jesus' *Book of Life*: for her salvation and also for her repentance.

I realized that just like I had entered into a life of knowing Jesus, she too could experience his love and healing. Luke 11:52 (NIV) says, "Woe to you experts in the law, because you have taken away the key to knowledge. You yourselves have not entered, and you have hindered those who were entering." I actually prayed this verse for both counsels on opposing sides, and lo and behold on August 3, 2008, God answered my prayer.

I entered my church, sat down in the back pew, and suddenly realized that the legal expert I had taken to the Law Society, Taxation Legal, and to court was sitting in front of me. God must have a sense of humor because He had directed her to my church!

I just had to speak with her. After the service she informed me of the baptism of her and her daughter two weeks previous and that she was looking for a home church. She concluded with, "I guess I was meant to come to Jesus after meeting you." She knew of my own belief in Jesus. After all, during our client/lawyer relationship, she needed an operation on her heart and she asked me to pray for her, which I did—in the name of Jesus.

We just have to believe that Jesus came to die on the cross for our sins and invite him into our hearts and our lives because he is so very generous to forgive us. He is so very generous to take away the sins of the world.

ॐ ॐ

So why am I so dedicated to testimony? The answer is simple: I've seen the good fruit that comes from giving testimony. Watching my family come to faith in a living Jesus and watching Jesus reveal himself again and again—changing lives, giving hope, revealing love, destroying whatever works Satan has done, and imparting new life—is why I am so dedicated to testimony. In other words, I've seen the evidence of faith.

Why Am I so Dedicated to Testimony?

* For a review of this chapter and to answer reflective questions, see the companion guide: *Preparing … The Testimony.*

BEFORE WE CONTINUE ON ...

I found myself early on in my Christian walk enamored by the power of testimony. I was astonished by how sharing a story about Jesus transformed people from a state of despair or even unbelief into a completely new creation. Oftentimes that person became alive and full of wonder, like a child who just couldn't get enough. I remember my atheist uncle driving something like *twelve* hours, from the United States up to my house in Alberta, Canada. Arriving at my door, in the dead of night, he exclaimed to me that he had been "born again." His energy was on high because his world was enlightened—he had been given a revelation of Jesus. I was completely amazed by his radical transformation.

I have had numerous friends and family members become Christians. Some of them have joined churches and some of them have chosen not to go that route, but each of them values Jesus. I can even look back to my days in high school and I am astounded by how many of us rebellious teenagers have fallen in love with Jesus. Is this coincidence? Of course not. The Holy Spirit is in the world; we are not alone in revealing Christ. Every seed we sow is the Holy Spirit's handiwork, and all our testimonies work together to reveal the truth about Jesus. However, I have learned over the years that there is a key to testifying. So for those who want to be ready to explain the hope that is in us,[32] remember this: when it comes to testimony, exemplifying Jesus—in *both* deeds and words—is the key that opens all hearts. With this in mind, it is time to move on to those misconceptions that have taken root in our Christian culture, regarding what a testimony is and what a testimony is not.

---

32. See 1 Pet 3:15-16: "Always be ready to make your defense to anyone who demands from you an accounting for the hope that is in you; yet do it with gentleness and reverence."

CHAPTER THREE

A Testimony is *Not* About God or Church

Let anyone with ears to hear listen!

—Mark 4:23

I have heard many Christian testimonies over the years. One of them brought me to believe in Jesus, others inspired me to draw closer to Jesus' Spirit, and others raised my faith so I would act in ways Jesus acted. However, unfortunately— and surprisingly—many didn't have any effect at all, except maybe for an emotional one.

Take for example Lori. Lori was planning on giving her testimony at our church's mom's group. She was also scheduled to give her testimony to our church's congregation on Easter Friday, so she needed to cut her story down. Lori asked if I would come to the mom's group and listen to her testimony, suggesting I take notes so she could get an idea of what parts to cut. I said I'd do it, but I wasn't sure what help I'd be. After all, I was still struggling, at this point, with writing my own testimony. I prayed to God that He would use me in some way to help Lori.

Well, the day proved to be an eye-opener for both Lori and me. As I sat listening to Lori's personal testimony, an uneasy feeling crept upon me. I tried focusing on taking notes; however, the uncomfortable feeling only grew. Soon I realized I deeply disliked my friend's testimony. *This doesn't make any sense,* I complained to God. *Lori is one of my friends. How can I be repelled by her very personal faith story?* By the end of my note taking, the answer as to why I felt so uncomfortable was clear. I wrote at the top of my page this verse: "For the testimony of Jesus is the spirit of prophecy" (Rev 19:10). Perhaps for added clarity, we should read this verse as stated in The Living Bible:

> Then I fell down at his feet to worship him [the angel], but he said, "No! Don't! For I am a servant of God just as you are, and as your brother Christians are, who testify of their faith in Jesus. Worship God. The purpose of all prophecy and of all I have shown you is to tell about Jesus." —*Rev 19:10, TLB*

This verse tells us the main purpose of prophecy is to tell about Jesus. In the New Testament, telling people about Jesus is what begins the transformational process of spiritual rebirth. But, surprisingly, through Lori's twenty-minute testimony, Jesus had not once been mentioned. Her faith story was about her detailed life experience, how she felt invisible to both people and to God. There were interesting and extremely heart wrenching details about her years

41

growing up and her experiences with marriage, but very little about Jesus. In fact, *Jesus was not even mentioned.* Her intense feelings of invisibility finally came to an end after she and her second husband found a wonderful church where she felt God's presence watching her. Because of this, "God" now felt real to her.[33]

After sitting down with Lori and revealing to her how I felt about her testimony and why, she was devastated. She couldn't believe she had forgotten to speak about Jesus. She was sure she had mentioned him. She scanned her story, but Jesus was nowhere to be found. Of course, Jesus was in her heart. Unfortunately, he was only somewhat on her mind; therefore, what she knew about him hadn't transferred to her story.

The fact was, no one had told Lori, a relatively new believer, what a Christian testimony was supposed to include. She had merely been asked to "share her testimony." She had never been taught to give deep thought as to how she had come to believe in Jesus or what she exactly believed. Lori could only assume her testimony was supposed to be about her life, how she came to believe in God, and how she began to attend church. Needless to say, after speaking with Lori, she set out straight away thinking about who she once thought Jesus to be and who she now believed him to be, and how God brought about that change. Her new story focuses only on those events that helped form her belief system, followed

---

33. I want to thank Lori who was so willing to share this experience, so we could learn from it.

by those events—including those supernatural events—that changed or expanded her belief system. In this following faith story, we now see God pursuing Lori, directing Lori, and ... finally, revealing Jesus to her. This is Lori's story.

Lori's Testimony

As a young girl I grew up believing I was worthless and invisible. Being rejected by my father and growing up in the shadow of my sister, the "golden girl" in everyone's eyes, I came to believe some kids just weren't worthy of affection. At age twelve I was raped. Discarded once again, this confirmed my belief that I was unlovable. Then one day I heard the piercing words, "Just ignore her. Pretend she's invisible." It was then I abandoned all thought of my life having any worth. My heart became bitterly hard and impenetrable.

Believing this lie drove me to the streets of Victoria at age fifteen. One night, a street mission house picked me up and brought me to church for an Easter service. Until then, my only experience with church was as a young girl, asked to sit still and face the front. The only significance of Jesus to me was in the majestic depictions on the stained glass windows, as I playfully ranked them most to least favorite. He was simply Jesus, God's son, who had lived two thousand years ago and died on a cross. End of story.

I can no longer remember the words preached during that Easter service, but the power I experienced through the message—which was most likely about Jesus having risen from the dead—will never fade. As I listened, I began to feel my numb, invisible body being lit up from the inside out. Then an intense warmth ran through me. I sensed my cloak of invisibility slowly being pulled away, leaving me unveiled in full view of everyone; yet, no one seemed startled over my sudden appearance. I felt powerful, reassuring, watchful eyes on me, but I didn't know whose they were. It would be another twenty-six years before I would understand the significance of this moment.

After getting married, my husband and I felt there had to be a deeper meaning to life than what we knew, so we decided to go back to church. Two years later, in a church in Saskatoon, Jesus finally began to reveal himself to me. It was during our first Sunday service at this church, during the message, that a flood of emotions began to pour through me. My heart, the one that had become so hardened from years of carrying pain, guilt, and shame, felt as if it were literally melting in my chest. Then words I will never forget flushed through me, "Lori, you are not an invisible, disposable person whom no one loves. I see you and you are mine. I am the Father you have been searching for." The emotions of the moment overtook me as I came to grips with the fact that there really was a "living" God who was supernaturally healing me. Tears began rolling down my face as my body filled with so much gratitude. I was getting a heart transplant.

I became thirsty to learn as much as I could about God after this experience. My husband and I began attending this church weekly; and through being discipled, I learned that God's son Jesus didn't just die on the cross—end of story.

But that he rose from the dead and is even now the mediator between God and myself. I also learned that Jesus is our healer. Jesus is the one who had known all my pain, heard every cry, and knew the horrible choices I had made in my life and still found me worthy enough to heal. God's restoring words that day also revealed to me whom the watchful eyes had belonged to years earlier. I now know that the Jesus I had confined to the stained glass windows of my church had actually been watching me and had been walking with me and will walk with me every moment of my life. I will never be out of his sight. I fell so much in love with Jesus for his amazing gift of restoration that I became thirsty to learn as much as I could about him. This desire has proved unquenchable.

๛ ๛

Obviously, Lori will not pull out this written story every time she speaks to someone about Jesus, but because she has now given deep thought to how her faith in Jesus began, she can better speak about it. The fact is, if we do not take time to meditate on who Jesus is and how we came to that knowledge, we will all at some point or another fall into the trap of speaking in general terms about "God" and perhaps end up describing our journey to finding "church."

But why, you may be asking yourself, is this even an issue? Why can't we speak about our love of God? The answer is, *of course you can speak about God.* However, when you are asked to give your testimony, or when a person asks you about your Christian faith, you must realize an extremely important task has been assigned to you, one that carries immense responsibilities: you have been asked to take the stand for Jesus.

Imagine yourself on the witness stand. Imagine a jury of both non-Christians and Christians alike eagerly waiting for your answer as this question is posed directly to you: "Who do you believe Jesus to be, and why do you believe it?" Of course, Satan is hoping you muddle things up, but you won't—not any more. After all, you've passed through a place of deep reflection. You know what you believe and why you choose to believe it. You are comfortable with being a Christian. And whether you have a lot of information to share, or a small amount of information to share, it won't matter because you are ready to speak.

Jesus Has Made God Known

Testifying about God rather than Jesus is the issue, by far, that I come across most often when reading or listening to testimonies. We tend to speak about God rather than Jesus, I think, for several reasons:

1. Because we love God immensely and believe in Him deeply, therefore our focus becomes God the Father and not Jesus who redeemed us.

2. Because we assume our audience is Christian (or, at the very least, familiar with Christianity), so we do not distinguish between the Trinity. (E.g., my audience knows that Jesus, the Spirit, and the Father are all united,

so I need not make a distinction between them or their unique purpose.)

3. We have simply not learned what a biblical testimony is, so we are ill equipped to share one.

4. We are uncomfortable speaking directly about Jesus. (E.g., speaking about Jesus is for the pastor of our church to do; I don't want to scare anyone away by speaking about Jesus.)

5. We fully associate Jesus with God—even though the world does not. Therefore, we unconsciously think we are speaking about Jesus even when we are not.

6. We know about Jesus, but we really haven't given our belief in him deep consideration.

Ultimately, when it comes to giving testimony we must remember God is invisible. He lives in unapproachable light:

It is he [God] alone who has immortality and dwells in unapproachable light, whom no one has ever seen or can see; to him be honor and eternal dominion. Amen. —*1 Tim 6:16*

And that Jesus has made God known:

No one has ever seen God. It is God the only Son, who is close to the Father's heart, who has made him known. —*Jn 1:18*

Speaking about God—without a revelation of Jesus—is like speaking about the unapproachable light. Our testimony may be appealing, emotional, and somewhat mystical, but it will not be bold, instructive, and life changing. God, after all, is that invisible, all-knowing, omnipresent being that, according to statistics, over eighty percent of people believe in. Whereas, Jesus is a man, a specific man whose life is rooted in history, and who is said to have died *and* risen from the grave. For an example of how the disciples handled "speaking about God," we can turn to the book of Acts.

A Biblical Testimony is Not about God—It's About Jesus

In Acts 17:16, we find Paul reaching out to the people in Athens, connecting with them through the idea of the "invisible God." But notice Paul does not stop with just the idea of God. He pushes in with a testimony of Christ saying, "You have been worshiping 'the unknown God' without knowing who he is":

> While Paul was waiting for them in Athens, he was deeply distressed to see that the city was full of idols. So he argued in the synagogue with the Jews and the devout persons, and also in the marketplace every day with those who happened to be there. Also some Epicurean and Stoic philosophers debated with him. Some said, "What does this babbler want to say?" Others said, "He seems to be a proclaimer of foreign divinities." (This was because he was telling the good news about Jesus and the resurrection.) So they took

him and brought him to the Areopagus and asked him, "May we know what this new teaching is that you are presenting? It sounds rather strange to us, so we would like to know what it means." Now all the Athenians and the foreigners living there would spend their time in nothing but telling or hearing something new.

Then Paul stood in front of the Areopagus and said, "Athenians, I see how extremely religious you are in every way. For as I went through the city and looked carefully at the objects of your worship, I found among them an altar with the inscription, 'To an unknown god.' What therefore you worship as unknown, this I proclaim to you. The God who made the world and everything in it, he who is Lord of heaven and earth, does not live in shrines made by human hands, nor is he served by human hands, as though he needed anything, since he himself gives to all mortals life and breath and all things. From one ancestor he made all nations to inhabit the whole earth, and he allotted the times of their existence and the boundaries of the places where they would live, so that they would search for God and perhaps grope for him and find him—though indeed he is not far from each one of us. For 'In him we live and move and have our being'; as even some of your own poets have said,

'For we too are his offspring.'

Since we are God's offspring, we ought not to think that the deity is like gold, or silver, or stone, an image formed by the art and imagination of mortals. While God has overlooked the times of human ignorance, now he commands all people everywhere to repent, because he has fixed a day on which he will have the world judged in righteousness by a man whom he has appointed, and of this he has given assurance to all by raising him from the dead."

When they heard of the resurrection of the dead, some scoffed; but others said, "We will hear you again about this." At that point Paul left them. But some of them joined him and became believers, including Dionysius the Areopagite and a woman named Damaris, and others with them. —*Acts 17:16-34*

If Paul had merely stated that God was indeed real and searching for Him was the very meaning of life, and that the Athenians were already worshiping God through the altar they had built, Paul would not have produced believers in God's Christ; he would have only encouraged the Greek's many pursuits. Instead, Paul pushed on with revelations of who Jesus is: the one who rose from the dead, appointed by God to be the judge of all. Many laughed and turned away. Yet

Paul was fruitful, as some wanted to hear more. Dionysius and Damaris came to Paul to hear more, and he brought them to believe in Jesus.

Similarly, in the story involving Cornelius (found in Acts 10) we are shown a man who loves God and is deeply loved by God. However, God does not leave Cornelius without a revelation of His Son:

> In Caesarea there was a man named Cornelius, a centurion of the Italian Cohort, as it was called. He was a devout man who feared God with all his household; he gave alms generously to the people and prayed constantly to God. One afternoon at about three o'clock he had a vision in which he clearly saw an angel of God coming in and saying to him, "Cornelius." He stared at him in terror and said, "What is it, Lord?" He answered, "Your prayers and your alms have ascended as a memorial before God. Now send men to Joppa for a certain Simon who is called Peter; he is lodging with Simon, a tanner, whose house is by the seaside." —*Acts 10:1-6*

God, in Cornelius' situation, was not content to leave Cornelius as is, with just a deep love for Himself—the invisible God—even though this is the first commandment: "You shall love the LORD your God with all your heart, and with all your soul, and with all your might" (Deut 6:5). This is because loving God encompasses a love for the *whole* of God, including His Son:

For the love of God is this, that we obey his commandments. And his commandments are not burdensome, for whatever is born of God conquers the world. *—1 Jn 5:3-4*

And this is his commandment, that we should believe in the name of his Son Jesus Christ and love one another, just as he has commanded us. *—1 Jn 3:23*

Cornelius was not yet introduced to the whole of God; therefore, an angel was dispatched to visit Cornelius so a Jewish man named Peter could be invited over to reveal to Cornelius what he was missing. Below is the testimony Peter gave Cornelius and his family:

Then Peter began to speak to them: "I truly understand that God shows no partiality, but in every nation anyone who fears him and does what is right is acceptable to him. You know the message he sent to the people of Israel, preaching peace by Jesus Christ—he is Lord of all. That message spread throughout Judea, beginning in Galilee after the baptism that John announced: how God anointed Jesus of Nazareth with the Holy Spirit and with power; how he went about doing good and healing all who were oppressed by the devil, for God was with him. We are witnesses to all that he did both in Judea and in Jerusalem. They put him to death by hanging him on a tree; but God raised him on the third day and allowed him to appear, not to all the people but to us who were chosen by God as witnesses, and who ate and drank with him after he rose from the dead. He commanded us to preach to the people and to testify that he is the one ordained by God as judge of the living and the dead. All the prophets testify about him that everyone who believes in him receives forgiveness of sins through his name." While Peter was still speaking, the Holy Spirit fell upon all who heard the word. —*Acts 10:34-44*

Peter explained to Cornelius about Jesus. As Cornelius and his family believed, the Holy Spirit baptized them to seal the truth of the revelation in their hearts. After this powerful introduction, Cornelius' love for God could be made complete. [34]

And so we must ask ourselves, "Are we telling the world about Jesus or about the invisible God? Do we speak clearly or in generalities?" We must focus our testimonies on who Jesus is—why? Because most people already believe in the invisible God. Our task, as Christians, is to reveal God's Son, Jesus, so that the Spirit of Everlasting Life can enter into, fall upon, anoint, baptize, and purify God's children, making the love of God complete.

* For a review of this chapter and to answer reflective questions, see the companion guide: *Preparing ... The Testimony.*

---

34. I do not mean to suggest that Cornelius now knew everything about God, but rather the whole of God's person (including Jesus and the Spirit) was introduced to Cornelius.

CHAPTER FOUR

A Testimony is *Not* About Faith

With great power the apostles gave their testimony to
the resurrection of the Lord Jesus, and great grace was
upon them all.

—Acts 4:33

The question is: *What do we mean when we speak about faith?* Do
we mean faith in ourselves? In God? Faith in that ambiguous
universe? Or, when we talk about "faith" do we mean we
should have faith in faith? We tend to fall into the comfortable
habit of speaking about our "faith" because either it is easy and
safe or we have forgotten the power that lies in speaking the
name of Jesus:

> There is salvation in no one else, for there is no other
> name under heaven given among mortals by which
> we must be saved. —*Acts 4:12*

Faith is always an easy answer: "My *faith* has gotten me
through. If it weren't for *faith*, I would have never made it.
Faith is very important to our family." However, faith without
a revelation of Jesus can mean anything. People will not

assume you are talking about faith in God's Son, Jesus. Also, speaking about faith in general will not direct the depressed, the hopeless, and the sincere God-seekers toward a concrete belief in the one who has the power to heal and renew. Having said this, however, we do need to speak about faith in order to stimulate conversation and learn about others: "Do you think faith is important? What is your faith?" For a personal example of a testimony dealing with the faith issue, I can use myself.

My "Faith" healed me!

In 2007 I was diagnosed with fibroids in my uterus. I prayed at that moment that if God would heal me then I would give testimony to my nurse and doctor. Well, I was healed. Read my following testimony and decide for yourself where my personal testimony falls short.

Faith Healing Testimony #1

A few years back, I suddenly became sick. I was tired. My hair was falling out. I was horribly depressed—I was a mess. I spent many nights crying my eyes out, asking God what was wrong with me. My husband noticed my poor state and urged me to see a doctor. My husband and I have been married for fourteen years; I am greatly blessed to have a husband as caring and attentive as he is. God introduced him to me one day at work. Since then, he has always been a strong and faithful support to me. I am so grateful to God for sending him. Following God, together, has been our absolute greatest journey.

During my illness I was attending university, working on my English degree. I feel called and anointed by God to write. But the studying was so difficult, especially with this illness—and with three young children to take care of on top of this! I have three girls. They're good but rather rambunctious, and so by seven o'clock every night I was exhausted. I figured my tiredness was due to my busyness, but my doctor, after conducting an ultrasound, told me I had fibroids in my uterus. He recommended a hysterectomy, depending on the fibroids' growth rate. Tired and sick, one day at a prayer service, held in my home church, I went forward for prayer. Three wonderful faith-filled ladies prayed for me to be healed. And I was. By faith we are truly healed! Our God is amazing!

ॐ ॐ

Let's now examine a faith healing testimony in the Bible. This is the story of the lame man sitting and begging at the Beautiful Gate:

> But Peter said, "I have no silver or gold, but what I have I give you; in the name of Jesus Christ of Nazareth, stand up and walk."[35] And he [Peter] took him by the right hand and raised him up; and immediately his feet and ankles were made strong. Jumping up, he stood

---

35. Notice how the apostles—even though they have no money to give—do not leave without giving this man something. Reminiscent of the verse Lk 11:41: "So give for alms those things that are within; and see, everything will be clean for you."

and began to walk, and he entered the temple with them, walking and leaping and praising God. All the people saw him walking and praising God, and they recognized him as the one who used to sit and ask for alms at the Beautiful Gate of the temple; and they were filled with wonder and amazement at what had happened to him. *—Acts 3:6-10*

Notice that if this story were to end here, the crowd would have been led to believe that God had somehow healed this man, since the man was praising God. However, the apostles, knowing a testimony is not about God, quickly moved in to explain how faith in Jesus accomplished the healing:

While he [the healed man] clung to Peter and John, all the people ran together to them in the portico called Solomon's Portico, utterly astonished. When Peter saw it, he addressed the people, "You Israelites, why do you wonder at this, or why do you stare at us, as though by our own power or piety we had made him walk? The God of Abraham, the God of Isaac, and the God of Jacob, the God of our ancestors has glorified his servant Jesus, whom you handed over and rejected in the presence of Pilate, though he had decided to release him. But you rejected the Holy and Righteous One and asked to have a murderer given to you, and you killed the Author of life, whom God raised from the dead. To this we are witnesses. And by faith in his name, his name itself has made this man strong, whom you see and know; and the faith that is through Jesus has given him this perfect health in the presence of all of you." —*Acts 3:11-16*

The Apostles were extremely clear as to the nature of this faith healing. They didn't need to go into detail about the man's life, since everyone was familiar with him, except to say he obviously couldn't walk and now he could. Most of their testimony was about who Jesus is: the Author of life, raised from the dead. They didn't let the glory fall to God. They instead told the crowd God has given His glory to Jesus. Peter and Paul, even though they talked about faith, described what their faith was *and* precisely whom it was in.

Based on the above example of a biblical faith healing testimony, I have since revised my testimony. By paying greater attention to the details that took place during the healing, more clarity is given and a stronger testimony emerges.

Faith Healing Testimony #2

In the year 2007, I began experiencing health issues. My menstruation cycle had become abnormally heavy. Oftentimes, it would come twice a month. I was extremely exhausted and my hair began falling out in clumps; plus, I was also depressed due to the ups and downs of hormone levels. My husband urged me to see my doctor. I did, and a physical exam revealed I had an enlarged uterus and extremely low iron levels, causing both my tiredness as well as my hair to fall out. My doctor then referred me to a radiologist, suspecting I had fibroids. After an ultrasound, my radiologist concluded I did indeed have fibroids in my uterus—three appeared on the ultrasound as well as a cyst. I was told I would need a hysterectomy in a year or so, depending on their rate of growth. My next appointment was scheduled for six months down the road, so the fibroids' growth rate could be measured.

Exactly six months later, I was at a prayer service held at the church my husband and I attended. In fact, I was on the prayer team. I was on the prayer team because I believe Jesus is alive; I believe he rose from the dead like the Bible says, and because he's God's Son—powerful just like God—we have hope for healing.

On this night, I was busy praying for a man when this thought popped into my head, "There is a woman who is depressed." Rather confused, I asked the man I was praying for, "Are you depressed?"

He said, "No."

I dismissed the thought and began praying for him again. Again the words, "There is a woman who is depressed" filled my mind. I asked the man, "Is your wife depressed?"

He replied, "Deidre, you know I'm not married."

I then realized *I* was the depressed woman, and the Holy Spirit was trying to get my attention. After all, I had been on the prayer team for the past six months; not once had I thought to ask for prayer for myself! I went to the others on the prayer team. I said, "I have fibroids in my uterus—I don't want them. Please pray for them to be gone."

Three women laid their hands upon me, and then they thanked God for his compassion and for sending Jesus. Then one of them said, "In the name of Jesus, I command you, fibroids, to dry up and be gone." Suddenly, a sharp pain shot through my stomach and I thought, "Holy cow, I think I'm healed!" However, I didn't tell anyone. I wanted to wait until after my next appointment to see if what I suspected was true.

The very next day, Monday, was my scheduled appointment. The nurse ran the ultrasound over me; except this time she looked rather confused. She continued with the scan for quite a while. Finally, she told me her machine seemed not to be working; she would have to conduct an internal ultrasound. After this second scan, she again looked confounded. The nurse then excused herself in order to speak with my doctor, who then also looked over the ultrasound. After a few whispers, the nurse turned to me and said, "I'm sorry Deidre, but the fibroids and the cyst seem to be gone. They're just not there anymore. Your uterus is normal."

My period, after this, went from lasting five days to a mere two days. My hair stopped falling out and my iron levels returned to normal. I had been healed just like others in the Bible were—in the name of Jesus. I believe Jesus truly is the Son of God with all power and authority in heaven *and* here on earth.

ॐ ॐ

A Testimony is *Not* About Faith

Between these two testimonies you will notice four things.

1St testimony	2nd testimony
Jesus is not identified.	Who I believe Jesus to be—God's Son, alive and able to help—is at the center of the story.
Too many inconsequential details are given.	Specific details regarding the healing help paint a picture of reality.
Glory is given first to my husband and then to three kind ladies and then to God.	The healing is tied to the Bible and to the person and nature of Jesus.
Three kind women healed me *by faith*.	It is clear that God has healed me, but it is also clear that He healed me through trust in His Son, Jesus.
	* Also notice, I am not hitting readers over the head with scripture verses. I am simply relaying my experience and describing how the experience relates to my belief in Jesus.

Believing that Jesus is God's Son, raised from the dead, is not an illogical belief; although, it may seem so to some at first glance. By presenting clear, bold testimonies—together—we can provide our jury with reasonable evidence as to the true nature of Jesus and his divine purpose. We can provide concrete reasons as to why we believe as we do.

However, now I must come clean. Because after telling God I would use my healing to testify to my nurse and doctor, the actual testimony I told them that day in the office went sadly like this, "My church prayed for me to be healed yesterday."

Yes. That is what I actually said to my doctor: "My church prayed for me to be healed yesterday." *Did my church heal me? Or perhaps some mysterious prayer healed me?* Unfortunately, a vague testimony such as the one I gave will leave an audience bewildered. But why did I give such an ambiguous testimony? Well, just before speaking to my nurse and doctor, I remember hesitating: sweat quickly collected in my armpits, my breathing became shallow. I was embarrassed and much too scared to speak the rather simplistic, yet strange, truth. I suspect my weak testimony left my listeners with the idea that some kind of "faith healing" had taken place. Faith healing, if we are not careful, can result in this type of belief: "I believed I could be healed and mysteriously I was—my self-belief healed me." When what actually happened was quite different: I was directed by God's Spirit to go for prayer and the fibroids were told—in the name of Jesus—to be gone. The fibroids literally obeyed the name of Jesus.

If you are preparing a healing testimony, it is also effective to provide evidence of that healing. In my case, ultrasound pictures or a doctor's medical notes. These are not difficult to get. Simply book an appointment and ask for a doctor to go over your file with you. A year after my own healing, I returned to my radiologist's office asking to go over my file.

My doctor took me through my ultrasound pictures, explaining medical terms to me and pointing out exactly what those pictures revealed. Together, we went over all possibilities: was I healed? Or, perhaps a mistake had been made and I never had fibroids in the first place, meaning the first ultrasound had somehow been compromised. Or, perhaps I was sick, but *not* with fibroids. The possibility of adenomyosis was discussed.[36] My doctor gave me his opinion on the validity of both a compromised ultrasound and adenomyosis—and why these possibilities were *not* likely candidates.

A compromised ultrasound picture was dismissed based on the fact that I went to see my family doctor because of certain health issues, such as hair falling out and unusual tiredness. Also, my doctor's physical exam testified to an enlarged uterus. In other words, all the signs for fibroids were there. Adenomyosis didn't fit the picture either, since it causes severe pain in the uterus, which I never experienced, and because, in most cases, hormone treatment is required for recovery. I was told that adenomyosis wouldn't clear up by itself, especially within a period of just six months. I then told my doctor exactly what had happened at the church that night and how I was healed.

I felt elated by this second visit. It was so much different from my first visit, where after being healed, I was terrified to speak (especially to an intelligent doctor who might think me crazy). But what in me had changed? *What happened to the fear and intimidation that once held me back?* The truth is, I had simply become comfortable with my own Christ-centered experience. I had gone through the situation, contemplated

---

36. Adenomyosis is a dysfunction of the uterus where the endometrium fails to release, causing severe build-up and pain.

it, and even written it out; then I had prayed for boldness.[37]

Consequently, at this second visit, I was able to speak openly with my doctor about what had happened to me in church and how exactly I was healed. I didn't preach. I simply shared my experience as clearly as I could. My doctor then shared with me a little bit about his lack of "religious experience." He then mentioned how he was quite happy that a real healing had taken place.[38]

Incidentally, I did tell my healing testimony again. I told it to my nineteen-year-old babysitter and long-time friend, Tessa. After hearing it, she burst out saying, "This is *sooo* big! You are talking about something being there and then suddenly not being there because of Jesus." The next day Tessa sat on my couch and said to me, "I'm ready. I'm ready to be a Christian. How do I do it?"[39] I had prayed for Tessa since the day I met her, when she was just eight years old. I began to purposefully testify to her a few years later. Through hearing many testimonies of Jesus, including my healing testimony, she now understands Jesus is alive and is her connection to God.

* For a review of this chapter and to answer reflective questions, see the companion guide: *Preparing ... The Testimony.*

---

37. Boldness is a fruit of the Spirit. See Chapter Six for the teaching on boldness.

38. Reminiscent of "For no one who does a deed of power in my name will be able soon afterward to speak evil of me" (Mk 9:39).

39. I do not mean to suggest that every time you share your testimony you will get a positive, thankful response. Sharing a testimony about Jesus can infuriate people.

CHAPTER FIVE

A Testimony is *Not* About Us

Those who believe in the Son of God have the
testimony in their hearts.

—1 John 5:10

Our Christian testimony centers upon a rather dramatic
and highly supernatural person. In other words, our
Christian testimony focuses upon someone other than
ourselves, someone who is very much different from us.
That extraordinary someone is Jesus: a man who has been
historically killed is—according to the testimonies given—
actually alive *and* he is the Son of God, who has made available
to all people the amazing Holy Spirit, the Spirit of Everlasting
Life. This rather strange supernatural truth, to which the
apostles testified, is the basis of testimony.[40] However, even
though this is our basis, the testimony of Jesus is not always
explained in two exact ways. Why is the testimony of Jesus
not told in the exact same way every time? Because each of

---

40. "And this is the testimony: God gave us eternal life, and this life is in
his Son" (1 Jn 5:11).

us is unique. Therefore, each of us brings to the table a new perspective, a new revelation about how the person of Christ affects us, teaches us, inspires us, or changes us. We speak about what we have *personally* seen and heard regarding Jesus, and these experiences are diverse.

To understand this better let's take a brief look at two of America's most prominent testimonies given in recent years: Mel Gibson's testimony which he entitled, *The Passion of The Christ* and William Paul Young's testimony entitled, *The Shack*. I bet these two testimonies were not what you were expecting me to pick as examples. For one, *The Passion of The Christ* isn't about Mel Gibson's life at all—it's completely about Jesus. But in all truth, it is about what Mel Gibson believes about Christ; it is his testimony. And it's powerful.

Just as powerful is Paul Young's *The Shack*, a book that became an international best seller on the *fiction* list. How can a fictional book be considered a testimony? The answer is simple: since a testimony is not primarily about us, author Paul Young can describe certain life-issues *fictionally* while still presenting the truth about Jesus. Paul's book is a story about a man whose life experience caused him to view God in a negative, unloving way. But when faced with certain truths about God, Jesus, and even the Spirit, this man found not just understanding but also a family who truly loved him. *The Passion* and *The Shack* are two completely different types of testimonies—both of which carry many revelations about Jesus. And that is what makes a testimony powerful—a revelation of Jesus.

A testimony is a story, a teaching, a song, a perspective that shares one, or two, or even numerous revelations (God-inspired truths) about Jesus. Sometimes, however, we lose focus. Sometimes we get muddled up. Sometimes we think testifying is all about us and our problems, our insecurities, or even our sin. We begin judging stories as "highly powerful" based on "best emotional baggage" or "most tragic event."

Just recently, for instance, I heard a disturbing story about a young girl who was asked to give her testimony in her local church. As the day on which she was to give her testimony approached, she came forward and told everyone she had been hoping for something bad to happen to her—so she could have a compelling testimony to tell. But, at the same time, she was too scared to really ask God to make something terrible happen. She was torn. She wanted to testify, but if a testimony was about surviving a horrible struggle or loss, then she wasn't sure she really wanted to testify.

This is where the church stands today, looking for emotional stories of life's struggles. The more damage we endure, the more seemingly powerful the story; the more tears we inspire, the more God *must* be working through our audience. In these types of stories, Jesus is often *unintentionally* left out because the high emotion of the story seemingly gives the story weight and importance. But the truth is, tragedy is not a prerequisite for giving testimony. Yes, tragedy is often part of a testimony, but it is not the main event. Getting to the revelation of Jesus—and describing how that revelation affects us—is the main event. In fact, every Christian can have an extraordinary testimony, even those who have lived peaceful lives.

To illustrate this, take for example my good friend Becky who once confided in me saying, "Your testimony is interesting and mine is boring. I've been a Christian since I was a little girl and have followed Jesus my whole life. Am I supposed to screw up and walk in sin in order for Jesus to dramatically rescue me, so that I, too, can have an interesting, head-turning testimony?" I assured Becky this wasn't the case. After all, this doesn't make much sense: walk in darkness so when Jesus shows up to rescue you, you'll be sure to have an emotionally spectacular testimony?

The issue here was that Becky's faith in Jesus had been built up slowly, over years, starting when she was just a small child. Because of this, she did not have a testimony that consisted of two neatly divided parts: a time before Jesus, plus a time after Jesus. These two time spans separated by one dramatic—and often tragic—event, all culminating in a revelation of Jesus. You may have seen this equation before, "My Life Before Jesus + My Life After Jesus = My Personal Testimony." However as Becky pointed out, this equation leaves her, a long-time Christian, *out* since she has never had a "Life before Jesus." Such a structure can also unintentionally place a testimony's emphasis on how "bad" a person has been in comparison to how "good" they are now. In other words, the worse the sin + the more dramatic the change = the more powerful the story, when the emphasis of a personal testimony should be on *who you believe Jesus to be, coupled with those events that worked to bring about—or strengthen—this revelation.*

Within the parameters of this new definition, Becky does indeed have a testimony. Her testimony will be about those truths she learned regarding Jesus and how she put those truths into action. In fact, Becky's testimony will most likely center upon, not how Jesus helped her to overcome a personal trial or tragedy, but how Jesus inspired her to help someone else. Or, she may even decide to use one of the many examples regarding how she lives her life by trusting Jesus to fulfill her needs/desires or how Jesus and the Holy Spirit personally directs her path. The truth is, we do not need to portray a life of sin and emotional scarring in order to have a spectacular testimony. Everybody's life is different, but we all encounter the same miraculous and compassionate Jesus. For an example of a long-time Christian's testimony, let's hear from my husband, DJ.

DJ's Testimony

I was raised in a Christian home, and I accepted what my parents taught me about God and Jesus at an early age. We were not an avid church-going family, but a family with parents and grandparents who knew the importance of having a relationship with God, believing that Jesus was the Son of God who died so our relationship with God could be restored. We were not a family that prayed together, but we were always willing to discuss God, Jesus, and the Bible if anyone raised the topic. We were not radical Bible-thumping evangelists, and we were probably somewhat distrustful of those who were. We were reserved Baptists who tried to live out our lives in kindness and helpfulness with Jesus and God quietly in the background.

Starting from this foundation, my personal faith began to grow when I was twelve years old and I made the commitment to God to read my Bible every day. It was wonderful how during my quiet times of reading that His words would speak to me, providing guidance. How one time I would read a passage and it was just words. Then, later on, I would reread the same passage and it was like a veil was lifted. All of a sudden I received an insight, a revelation, a new understanding. The revelations were exciting and made me feel special and thankful. Through these daily devotionals my knowledge of the Bible increased and I learned that answers could be sought by praying and reading God's word.

In university I continued my learning by participating in Bible studies and seminars. During this period, I began to discover that there is a spiritual battle going on around us and for us. I started to read about different spiritual battles Christians had gone through. One book that really impacted me was Michael Warnke's *The Satan Seller*. It was an autobiography that told how he got involved in Satanism and how Jesus delivered him. Little did I know this awareness, which seemed so "unreal" that I half-heartedly believed it, was soon all going to come into play.

God's hand was upon the relationship between my wife Deidre and me from the beginning. We were very much polar opposites; so, on our second date, I asked God in my head, "Lord, why am I here?" It was at this time that Deidre told me about her nightmares. When she was done, I heard a voice in my head say, "They are demonic … that is why you are here. You are here to help her." I had never heard God's voice before, but I recognized it right away! Over the next few weeks I found myself in a spiritual battle. The Holy Spirit helped me recognize the presence of the demonic and, thankfully, also gave me peace. I was not afraid. And when the demonic attacked, I found myself drawing upon the name of Jesus to make the demons back off. Suddenly the doubt about such things as Michael Warnke's autobiography, including Satan and demons, was gone. Eventually, once Deidre was ready, the demonic was cast out of her body. Over the next four years, we battled for her restoration and worked to sever the claims that the demonic had made over her and our unborn children.

Through this all God answered a specific prayer of mine. A prayer made in my early twenties, a prayer to bless me with a wife who was strong in faith, one who would pray with me. He transformed Deidre into this person.

I grew up seeing Christianity as a moral code; now, after everything Jesus has shown me, I see Christianity as being a supernatural life. A spiritual world exists all around us, and Jesus is there in control of it all.

৯৯ ৯৯

Dealing with Tragedy and Sin

Although a testimony is primarily about Jesus and what we know and have experienced regarding him, information about our oftentimes tragic or colorful pasts, prior to a discovery or revelation of Jesus, frequently must be included in our story simply because it played a chief role in our spiritual journey. In other words, our past should be there with a clear purpose. Such a purpose might include: describing a tragic past event in order to show what parts of your life Jesus has healed, or using a past event to help explain how your initial (positive or negative) belief in God and Jesus developed.

Your testimony might also include speaking about past sinful actions in order to clarify why you felt the need to receive forgiveness and why you believe Jesus is able to forgive your sin. Also, depending upon a person's situation, a description of a past life can be used to highlight a complete change of direction, *after* Jesus has been revealed. Take for example the following two stories, one from a woman named Adriana B. and one from the Apostle Paul. In both stories past sin is discussed—but for Adriana and Paul, the discussion of the past serves to highlight Jesus as being the one who both forgives and brings redemption, as well as new life.

Testimony #1 – It's Not About Adriana B. It's About What She's "Seen and Heard."

I have always believed in God. I thought of Him as an ominous ruler sitting on a golden throne, scowling as He doled out punishment for sin. I remember nights as a child terrified I was going to hell. At the age of five, a neighbor girl sexually abused me numerous times; afterwards, I initiated the same thing with others. This sinful behavior continued until the age of ten when I finally decided to stop. I felt like a dirty disgusting piece of garbage—not good enough to go to heaven. Then at summer Bible camp I heard Jesus came to earth to die for our sins, so it no longer mattered that I wasn't perfect. I was told if I prayed "Jesus, come into my heart and be my savior" I would go to heaven. After I prayed this I felt physically and mentally different—I felt happy. For a while afterwards, I wasn't as afraid of going to hell.

Religious life was difficult. I found church services boring. The things that were taught fueled my belief that God was scary and that one day He would send me to hell. As soon as I was old enough to make my own choices, church stopped. Family life was difficult too. Being the only adopted child in a family of seven, I never truly felt like part of the family. After all, my siblings often told me that I wasn't really one of them. My self-worth had always come from the acceptance of others and, therefore, I worked hard to excel at things: I got high marks, won awards and tried to be everyone's best friend. I hoped these accomplishments would make my parents proud, but instead my siblings resented me even more, attributing my successes to being adopted, and therefore spoiled. I hated to be alone. I remember feeling stressed after sleepovers thinking I would come home to an empty house—*finally, the family had decided to leave me.*

In my late twenties, I felt completely rejected by my husband. He chose drinking, friends, and the bar over me, often leaving me alone with our new daughter. I felt my marriage was a nightmare. I wanted to walk away so many times. During this time, I had a falling out with my best friend and was rejected once again. One Sunday morning, I woke up consumed by sadness. Suddenly, a thought popped into my head: "Try your friend Tanya's church." So I went.

I panicked when the music started playing. It was a rock band—*so disrespectful*. However, the service was filled with passion. The message that day was all about personal relationships and God's expectations of us as we interact with one another. All the emotions and thoughts I had about my marriage and friendships were addressed that morning. I have since been involved in small groups (meetings to learn about the Bible), made Christian friends, and have attended Christian conferences. Nine years ago, my husband and I attended a Marriage Encounter (a Christian course that helps partners rediscover their marriage). There we saw examples of what a marriage looks like when Jesus is present and when he is not. We committed our lives and marriage to Jesus that weekend. I take great comfort that my husband now feels that he is accountable to God and I know that Jesus directs both of our paths.

My new Christian experiences combined with my Catholic upbringing have all helped to teach me the truth about Jesus. Jesus takes away the fear of hell; he directs my path when I need help; he accepts me as is. I no longer fear

God. He is my "papa" and Jesus is my brother. I have a family who will never reject me!

Although I asked for forgiveness many times for my childhood sexual experiences, I continued to carry huge amounts of shame and guilt. I felt my actions could be forgiven but not ever forgotten. Recently, at an evening service at our church, I stood with my hands stretched out praying to not only be forgiven for this sin but also that I would no longer feel the shame. I prayed that God would replace this humiliation in my heart with His Holy Spirit. I prayed repeatedly, "Take away this burden, forgive this sin, and fill me with Your Spirit!" Suddenly, a woman from the prayer team placed her hands on my face and a bolt of lightning went through me causing me to "yelp." After this, I shook uncontrollably for the rest of the service. I may not know exactly what happened that night, but I do know this ... I now feel as though God has not only forgiven me but has freed me from the defeating thoughts that held me in constant guilt. A few days after this experience I was able to, for the first time, write this testimony to Jesus being completely honest about my past. "For I will forgive their wickedness and will remember their sins no more" (Heb 8:12, NIV).

Testimony #2 – It's Not About Paul. It's About What He's "Seen and Heard."

In the following verses, Paul, after being accused by the Jewish leaders for agitating the people with his teaching, defiling the temple (by supposedly bringing Greeks into it[41]), and for declaring the resurrection of the dead (which Sadducees disagreed with) was arrested and taken to King Agrippa. It was here where Paul gave his personal testimony about Jesus. First, Paul spoke about his sin (the murder of Christian men and women); however, Paul's sin is not the center of the story. Paul's testimony is a revelation of Jesus as the resurrection (which Pharisees such as Paul firmly hoped for). Paul's mention of past sin was spoken about simply to reveal Paul's complete change of direction, now that Jesus had been revealed to him:[42]

> Agrippa said to Paul, "You have permission to speak for yourself." Then Paul stretched out his hand and began to defend himself: "I consider myself fortunate that it is before you, King Agrippa, I am to make my defense today against all the accusations of the Jews, because you are especially familiar with all the customs and controversies of the Jews; therefore I beg of you to listen to me patiently. All the Jews know my way of life from my youth, a life spent from the beginning among my own people and in Jerusalem. They have known for a long time, if they are willing to testify, that I have belonged to the strictest sect of

---

41. See Acts 21:27-29.

42. Paul's complete change of direction is evidence that he really did see Jesus alive. Meeting Jesus deeply affected him, and it changed the course of his life.

our religion and lived as a Pharisee.[43] And now I stand here on trial on account of my hope in the promise made by God[44] to our ancestors, a promise that our twelve tribes hope to attain, as they earnestly worship day and night. It is for this hope, your Excellency, that I am accused by Jews! Why is it thought incredible by any of you that God raises the dead? Indeed, I myself was convinced that I ought to do many things against the name of Jesus of Nazareth. And that is what I did in Jerusalem; with authority received from the chief priests, I not only locked up many of the saints in prison, but I also cast my vote against them when they were being condemned to death. By punishing them often in all the synagogues I tried to force them to blaspheme; and since I was so furiously enraged at them, I pursued them even to foreign cities.

With this in mind, I was traveling to Damascus with the authority and commission of the chief priests, when at midday along the road, your Excellency, I saw a light from heaven, brighter than the sun, shining around me and my companions. When we had all fallen to the

---

43. A Pharisee observed doctrine and commandments strictly; they believed in the survival of souls after death, and in resurrection of the body, and they were influential with the Jewish public. Sadducees believed the soul died with the body; they only followed the written law and not traditions. The Zealots believed in accordance with the Pharisees, but had an overwhelming desire to be free from foreign leadership, considering God to be their only true leader. See Maier, *Josephus*, 265-266.

44. Paul's hope is in resurrection after death.

ground, I heard a voice saying to me in the Hebrew language, 'Saul, Saul, why are you persecuting me? It hurts you to kick against the goads.'[45] I asked, 'Who are you, Lord?' The Lord answered, 'I am Jesus whom you are persecuting. But get up and stand on your feet; for I have appeared to you for this purpose, to appoint you to serve and testify to the things in which you have seen me and to those in which I will appear to you.[46] I will rescue you from your people and from the Gentiles—to whom I am sending you to open their eyes so that they may turn from darkness to light and from the power of Satan to God, so that they may receive forgiveness of sins and a place among those who are sanctified by faith in me.'" —*Acts 26:1-18*

Paul's testimony contains two revelations. The first is that the resurrection of the dead begins with Jesus, who rose from the dead and appeared to him on the road to Damascus.[47] For Paul, his great hope in God's promise of eternal life was completely confirmed when Jesus revealed himself. Paul's second revelation is that Jesus, being the Messiah, is able to forgive sin (even Paul's sin of blasphemy, torture, and corrupt

---

45. "Kick against the goads" is an old adage. A "goad" is a cattle prod used to direct cattle in a certain direction. If an animal were to kick against a goad (goads are usually sharp), it would only hurt itself. Modern-day goads are electrically charged. This implies Jesus had been prodding Paul to go in a certain direction, but Paul was fighting against him.

46. Or, "For I have appeared to you to appoint you as my servant and witness. You are to tell the world what you have seen and what I will show you in the future" (Acts 26:16, NLT).

47. The resurrection is one of both body and soul. See 1 Cor 15:44.

judgment[48]).

Ultimately, if our Christian testimony is primarily about us and our lives—without a revelation of Jesus—then the story with the most emotional ups and downs will seem strongest. But, if a testimony is about *who* Jesus is, and *how* we came to and *grew* in that knowledge, and even how that knowledge moves us to *affect* others in our world, then all of our testimonies, including Christians who once lived without Jesus as well as those who believed in Jesus all their lives, can be of equal strength and value.

* For a review of this chapter and to answer reflective questions, see the companion guide: *Preparing ... The Testimony.*

---

48. Paul considered himself to be a blasphemer. See 1 Tim 1:13. He blasphemed Jesus by speaking wrongly about him and because he persecuted Jesus' followers.

BEFORE WE CONTINUE ON …

I have given many testimonies over the years, yet I am not a pastor or a preacher. In fact, I have no official "ministry" to speak of. Truth be told, at present time, I don't even attend church. For me, Jesus is just life. He is the reality of the cosmos—all things made in him and through him. Because of this, I find it hard to reduce him to mere "religion." In fact, I dislike the word *religion*, since it does so little to actually describe the deep satisfaction and love I receive from God, from Jesus, and from the Holy Spirit.

I didn't always feel this way, of course. It takes only moments for me to recollect how "lost" I was before I came to an understanding of Christ, but really lost is the wrong word. It was more like I had amnesia. It was like I had no idea of who I was, or where I had come from, or who loved me and cherished me. I had forgotten I had a spiritual family, and so I acted as a lost little orphan: sad, distressed, looking for love, and always wary of the world around me. However, I did suspect I had a spiritual family, and for me this is where my faith in Jesus began—with a desire to find and know the invisible God.

During the early stage of my journey, I had no idea Jesus would play such a significant role in my awakening and I had absolutely zero understanding of the Holy Spirit. When I became a Christian, I slowly awoke from my amnesia. Through drowsy eyes I saw the shadowy figures of a family around me, cheering me on. As I fully awoke, I found unconditional love, true comfort, and a home. I now realize where I come from, who I am, and why I was created: "For we are what he has made us, created in Christ Jesus for good works, which God prepared beforehand to be our way of life" (Eph 2:10).

I was transformed, not by rules, nor by a mere belief, nor by some unknowable supernatural power, but by the love of family. This family—Father, Spirit, and Son—has taught me how to love, how to help others, and how to depend on them for guidance and worth. However, this education (*or this discipleship*) that I received didn't happen overnight, nor is it complete (trust me, I still have a lot to learn).

To me, my life is a testimony about Jesus and testimony is my life. Because of this, I understand the immense importance of continually strengthening my own testimony. *How do we strengthen our testimonies?* The answer is relatively simple:

- Be willing to *Live The Testimony*.

CHAPTER SIX

What is a Strong Christian Testimony?

For in Christ Jesus neither circumcision nor uncircumcision counts for anything; the only thing that counts is faith working through love.

—Galatians 5:6

A Christian testimony should be in constant revelation. After all, as we walk with Jesus, he will reveal more and more of himself to us. This will, in turn, strengthen our faith. And our faith, when acted upon, will produce evidence, thereby strengthening our testimonies.

Every Christian has a revelation of Jesus. Most Christians begin their Christian walk with a revelation of Jesus as hope. In a world with sometimes little or no hope, Jesus becomes the life raft that saves us. Jesus gives hope for a future after death and hope for a better future now, here on earth. However, if this is where our experience with Jesus ends, then this is all Jesus will be to us—our hope of attaining a better life. And even though this revelation is both wonderful and foundational, there is so much more to Jesus.

Ultimately, the strongest testimonies come from Christians who live to learn about Jesus and engage in active faith, all while submitting to love. A *strong* Christian testimony then is one that continually grows in the knowledge of Jesus, continually shares that knowledge boldly, while at the same time performs good works based on Jesus' teaching of love— all while abstaining from works of darkness. Because a biblical testimony deals not only with our belief system, but also with the way we conduct our whole lives, our Christian testimony becomes our most valuable asset—it is life itself.

Our testimonies then are far more important than any of us, in our western culture, give them credit for. To understand the immense significance of our Christian testimonies, and why we should work at strengthening them and expanding them, let's break down the definition I gave and examine each section.

Are You Living The Testimony?

> "A strong Christian testimony is one that continually grows in the knowledge of Jesus, continually shares that knowledge boldly, while at the same time performs good works based on Jesus' teaching of love—all while abstaining from works of darkness."

1. "Continually grows in the knowledge of Jesus Christ."
Growing in the knowledge of Jesus requires more than just a Bible and an hour of peace, though reading the Bible is a large part of it. Growing requires learning coupled with experience. This process is called discipleship. A disciple is one who literally leaves her way of life behind in order to follow a teacher expressly for the purpose of being taught.

Baptism is often the defining line between the world with all its desires and the life of a dedicated disciple of Jesus. In other words, after dedicating herself or himself to the Father, the Spirit, and the Son, the disciple's desire to become like her teachers begins to outweigh everything else in her life. In the New Testament, Jesus' disciples went through a period of intense learning (and, yes, there was much failing involved). After Jesus' disciples became "Spirit-filled," they were then sent out and they made new disciples themselves. These new disciples then dedicated themselves to a period of learning:

> So those who welcomed his [Peter's] message were baptized, and that day about three thousand persons were added. They devoted themselves to the apostles' teaching and fellowship, to the breaking of bread and the prayers. —Acts 2:41-42

Discipleship, therefore, is not periodic in-class learning, like taking a night class once a week. It is continuous on-the-job training. Being a disciple of Jesus means learning (over time) to let go of distractions in order to dedicate one's self to learning about Jesus and his teachings, much like Mary and the other disciples dedicated themselves:

> Now as they went on their way, he [Jesus] entered a certain village, where a woman named Martha welcomed him into her home. She had a sister named Mary, who sat at the Lord's feet and listened to what he was saying. But Martha was distracted by her many tasks; so she came to him and asked, "Lord, do you not care that my sister has left me to do all the work by myself? Tell her then to help me." But the Lord answered her, "Martha, Martha, you are worried and distracted by many things; there is need of only one thing. Mary has chosen the better part, which will not be taken away from her." —*Lk 10:38-42*

Unfortunately, "doing" is often viewed by our culture as being more helpful than "listening and learning." Because of this, service can sometimes overshadow discipleship and discipline. As Christians, we may feel more valued if we can be of service to Jesus, or to an organized ministry. But I can personally attest to the enormous value of building a strong interior foundation by seeking and listening to the Father, the Spirit, and the Son *before* jumping into the world of service. Fortunately for us all, when it comes to learning, there are many ways a disciple can learn, and for this diversity we should be thankful. The following sources are listed so we may be open to all the ways in which God delivers His teachings.

Forms of Spiritual Teaching

a. From the Bible:

One obvious source of learning is the Bible. After all, the Old Testament was written by those who prophesied, by the person of the Holy Spirit, about Jesus and also about events to come; whereas, the New Testament was written primarily by those who had "seen and heard" events from the beginning of Jesus' ministry. Therefore, these two sources contain a vast amount of wonderful and important information regarding Jesus and the spiritual life. However, sometimes we allow the Bible to replace the Holy Spirit. Consequently, instead of developing a relationship with the Spirit and with Jesus, we attempt to build a relationship with the Bible. By valuing the book over the persons who inspired it, we risk building an idol out of a book. While ironically, the Bible itself calls us into relationship with the persons of the Trinity.

b. From Jesus:

Jesus is obviously not living amongst us in bodily form today as he was in Mary's day; therefore, we cannot simply do like Mary did and go to Jesus to sit at his feet. But we can still learn from Jesus. After all, Jesus is not dead. He has been resurrected. He is alive. Paul, as well as many other disciples, learned in this fashion—directly from Jesus:

> Then he [Jesus] appeared to more than five hundred brothers and sisters at one time, most of whom are still alive, though some have died. Then he appeared

to James, then to all the apostles. Last of all, as to
one untimely born, he appeared also to me [Paul].
—*1 Cor 15:6-8*

For I want you to know, brothers and sisters, that the
gospel that was proclaimed by me [Paul] is not of
human origin; for I did not receive it from a human
source, nor was I taught it, but I received it through a
revelation of Jesus Christ. —*Gal 1:11-12*

Now there was a disciple in Damascus named
Ananias. The Lord said to him in a vision, "Ananias."
He answered, "Here I am, Lord." The Lord said to him,
"Get up and go to the street called Straight, and at
the house of Judas look for a man of Tarsus named
Saul. At this moment he is praying, and he has seen
in a vision a man named Ananias come in and lay
his hands on him so that he might regain his sight."
—*Acts 9:10-12*

Granted, learning directly from Jesus is not (at present
time) the standard, though I have heard a handful of stories
where people were spoken to by Jesus in a vision or a dream.
However, thankfully, we can also learn in other ways.

c. From Preachers:

But Paul and Barnabas remained in Antioch, and there, with many others, they taught and proclaimed the word of the Lord. *—Acts 15:35*

d. From Prophets:

At that time prophets came down from Jerusalem to Antioch. One of them named Agabus stood up and predicted by the Spirit that there would be a severe famine over all the world; and this took place during the reign of Claudius. The disciples determined that according to their ability, each would send relief to the believers living in Judea; this they did, sending it to the elders by Barnabas and Saul. *—Acts 11:27-30*

e. From all members of the Church:

Now there are varieties of gifts, but the same Spirit; and there are varieties of services, but the same Lord; and there are varieties of activities, but it is the same God who activates all of them in everyone. To each is given the manifestation of the Spirit for the common good. *—1 Cor 12:4-7*

Developing in areas of spiritual gifts, services, and activities is a highly personal journey. It is a journey that is not always understood by those around us, even if they are Christians. To make matters more muddied, oftentimes churches are not open to embracing all the gifts. Consequently, we may feel discouraged. For instance, healing may be looked at as "not for today," prophecy may scare many, gifted teachers may need to pursue degrees in order to be taken seriously, and the service of pastor may be perceived as "man's work." But be encouraged, the Holy Spirit will open doors for all of us to participate with an honor that comes from knowing Christ—and Christ alone. Keep in mind though, not all of us will work or volunteer within a church building. The Spirit leads us to all sorts of places; we get dispersed like embers from a fire, spread throughout the world, sometimes as janitors, as film makers, or as housewives and managers. Wherever we are, there is our ministry.

So let's remember, spiritual gifts and places of service are great, they remind us that God values each one of us individually, and that He created us as both unique as well as helpful, but developing in maturity and love is far more important. Love helps us to be patient and understanding, and maturity helps us to trust the Holy Spirit to worry about where and how we will serve.

f. Lastly (and most importantly), from the Spirit:
In all actuality, the only way we can be true disciples of Jesus is by having the anointing of Jesus' Spirit, who constantly teaches us: directing us to listen, confirming what we hear, changing our minds about pre-conceived ideas, speaking to us, and leading us into experience. Ultimately, when Jesus

left earth to return to his Father, he didn't leave us alone. He sent his Spirit to lead and teach us. Therefore, God is literally on earth—we are not alone. We have a teacher who knows everything: from science, to history, to the arts, to spiritual teaching. And although this may be difficult to accept, it is possible for Christians to have the same close and intimate relationship with the Holy Spirit that the early apostles and disciples shared with Jesus. The Spirit is our friend and our teacher:

> And we speak of these things in words not taught by human wisdom but taught by the Spirit, interpreting spiritual things to those who are spiritual. —1 Cor 2:13

> I write these things to you concerning those who would deceive you. As for you, the anointing that you received from him [Jesus] abides in you, and so you do not need anyone to teach you. But as his anointing teaches you about all things, and is true and is not a lie, and just as it has taught you, abide in him. —1 Jn 2:26-27

> When they bring you before the synagogues, the rulers, and the authorities, do not worry about how you are to defend yourselves or what you are to say; for the Holy Spirit will teach you at that very hour what you ought to say. —Lk 12:11-12

Finally, growing continually in the knowledge of Jesus Christ also has to do with experience. After all, the books of the New Testament are, for the most part, not teaching notes, but a description of spiritual experience. Spiritual experience often comes as we trust Jesus and learn to follow the Spirit, engaging in activities that please God. My most significant experiences, those that revealed to me the reality of the spiritual world, the significance of Jesus, and the person of the Spirit, came as I simply reached out to tell people about Jesus and also during times of prayer. However, being a disciple of Jesus is not easy. After all, learning is not easy. Listening as well as understanding does not come easily to any of us, especially if we allow a worldly life to distract us—and don't we all get distracted from time to time? Unfortunately, like any good habit, being a disciple requires dedication to the learning process:

> About this [Jesus] we have much to say that is hard to explain, since you have become dull in understanding. For though by this time you ought to be teachers, you need someone to teach you again the basic elements of the oracles of God. —Heb 5:11-12

2. "Continually shares that knowledge boldly."

Boldness is frankness, an unashamed clarity in any situation because of a complete lack of fear.[49] Boldness is not rude or pushy. It is simply clarity in speech and action based on

---

49. "Courage," on the other hand, means doing something despite fear.

those things that we *know* to be true. The Bible continually encourages us to be bold disciples of Jesus. But why should we be bold and how do we get bold? Spiritual boldness, the kind that destroys fear, the kind the early disciples and apostles walked in, begins with prayer simply because it comes from the Holy Spirit:

> When they had prayed, the place in which they were gathered together was shaken; and they were all filled with the Holy Spirit and spoke the word of God with boldness. —*Acts 4:31*

> Pray also for me, so that when I speak, a message may be given to me to make known with boldness the mystery of the gospel, for which I am an ambassador in chains. Pray that I may declare it boldly, as I must speak. —*Eph 6:19-20*

> At the same time pray for us as well that God will open to us a door for the word, that we may declare the mystery of Christ, for which I am in prison, so that I may reveal it clearly, as I should. —*Col 4:3-4*

As disciples, we are expected to speak boldly and clearly because of our confidence in who Jesus is:

> Since, then, we have such a hope [as Jesus], we act with great boldness, not like Moses, who put a veil over his face to keep the people of Israel from gazing

at the end of the glory that was being set aside.[50]

—2 Cor 3:12-13

To study the immense importance of spiritual boldness, we can turn to the book of Acts. It is here where the apostles and disciples, now filled with the Spirit of God, are working to quickly spread the message of salvation through belief in Jesus. However, because of Peter and John's testifying and teaching, and their healing of a lame man "in the name of Jesus," the rulers, elders, and scribes grew quickly troubled and had Peter and John arrested:

> They said, "What will we do with them? For it is obvious to all who live in Jerusalem that a notable sign has been done through them; we cannot deny it. But to keep it from spreading further among the people, let us warn them to speak no more to anyone in this name." So they called them and ordered them not to speak or teach at all in the name of Jesus. But Peter and John answered them, "Whether it is right in God's sight to listen to you rather than to God, you must judge; for we cannot keep from speaking about what we have seen and heard." After threatening them again, they let them go, finding no way to punish them because of the people, for all of them praised God for what had happened. For the man on whom this sign

---

50. The "end of glory" that was being "set aside" was the Old Covenant, established through Moses. See 2 Cor 3:7-11 for "the ministry of the Spirit" which is the New Covenant.

of healing had been performed was more than forty years old. —*Acts 4:16-22*

It was immediately after this experience of intimidation that Peter and John sought out their friends. Notice what it was their friends did in order to counteract the attempted silencing of Peter and John:

After they were released, they went to their friends and reported what the chief priests and the elders had said to them. When they heard it, they raised their voices together to God and said, "Sovereign Lord, who made the heaven and the earth, the sea, and everything in them, it is you who said by the Holy Spirit through our ancestor David, your servant: 'Why did the Gentiles rage, and the peoples imagine vain things? The kings of the earth took their stand, and the rulers have gathered together against the Lord and against his Messiah.' For in this city, in fact, both Herod and Pontius Pilate, with the Gentiles and the peoples of Israel, gathered together against your holy servant Jesus, whom you anointed, to do whatever your hand and your plan had predestined to take place. And now, Lord, look at their threats, and grant to your servants to speak your word with all boldness, while you stretch out your hand to heal, and signs and wonders are performed through the name of your holy servant Jesus." When they had prayed, the place in which they were gathered together was shaken; and

they were all filled with the Holy Spirit and spoke the
word of God with boldness. —*Acts 4:23-31*

Boldness is a necessity of the gospel. We absolutely need
the boldness of the Holy Spirit in order to overcome fear and
intimidation. Boldness is not aggression. It is the removal of
fear, along with complete clarity in teaching and testifying—
no matter the situation. If you want to understand boldness,
simply begin by praying for boldness. The Spirit will teach
you.

3. "Performs good works based on Jesus' teaching of love."

As I mentioned before, a testimony is made up of both our
deeds and words. Therefore, for the person who has entered
into covenant relationship with God (Father, Spirit, and Son)
their deeds and words should not be done in vain—that is,
without love:

If I speak in the tongues of mortals and of angels, but do
not have love, I am a noisy gong or a clanging cymbal.
And if I have prophetic powers, and understand all
mysteries and all knowledge, and if I have all faith,
so as to remove mountains, but do not have love, I
am nothing. If I give away all my possessions, and if
I hand over my body so that I may boast, but do not
have love, I gain nothing. —*1 Cor 13:1–3*

95

If we think back to book one (*Studying ... The Testimony*) and recall the meaning of vain, "to do something in a useless, unfruitful, lacking substance, futile, foolish way," we realize that the very meaning of "vain" is to "gain nothing." We may call ourselves Christians or disciples of Jesus, we may even be working or preaching in a ministry, but without love—we work in vain. Love is the highest calling of a Christian. Love is the "good fruit" of the Holy Spirit:

> The fruit of the Spirit is love, joy, peace, patience, kindness, generosity, faithfulness, gentleness, and self-control. —*Gal 5:22-23*

> You did not choose me but I chose you. And I appointed you to go and bear fruit, fruit that will last, so that the Father will give you whatever you ask him in my name. —*Jn 15:16*

> On that day many will say to me, "Lord, Lord, did we not prophesy in your name, and cast out demons in your name, and do many deeds of power in your name?" Then I will declare to them, "I never knew you; go away from me, you evildoers." —*Mt 7:22-23*

Our goal as disciples is to bring honor to the holy name of God by walking as Jesus walked—in the love of God:

As the Father has loved me, so I have loved you; abide in my love. —*Jn 15:9*

Owe no one anything, except to love one another; for the one who loves another has fulfilled the law. The commandments, "You shall not commit adultery; You shall not murder; You shall not steal; You shall not covet"; and any other commandment, are summed up in this word, "Love your neighbor as yourself." Love does no wrong to a neighbor; therefore, love is the fulfilling of the law. —*Rom 13:8-10*

For the disciple who desires to be like Jesus, who learns to obey the Holy Spirit, and who has endeavored to set herself or himself apart from vain deeds—choosing instead to abide in the love of Christ and do the works of Christ—the end result is complete boldness on the final day of judgment:

Love has been perfected among us in this: that we may have boldness on the day of judgment, because as he is, so are we in this world. There is no fear in love, but perfect love casts out fear; for fear has to do with punishment, and whoever fears has not reached perfection in love. —*1 Jn 4:17-18*

But what exactly are the "works of Christ"? Is it preaching? Is it feeding the poor? Is it miraculous healing? Is it volunteering our time? What is it that we as disciples of Christ should be doing?

Examples of Good Works:

> Then they said to him, "What must we do to perform the works of God?" Jesus answered them, "This is the work of God, that you believe in him whom he has sent." —Jn 6:28-29

- Offer a sacrifice of praise by confessing his name (Heb 13:15).
- Give alms from those things that are within (Lk 11:41).[51]
- Care for orphans and widows (Jas 1:27).
- Be generous and ready to share (1 Tim 6:18).
- In teaching show integrity, so no one will have anything evil to say of you (Titus 2:7-8).
- Meet urgent needs (Titus 3:14).
- Sell your possessions and give alms (Lk 12:33).
- Bring back a sinner from wandering (Jas 5:19-20).
- Have mercy (compassion and forgiveness) on others (Jude 1:22).
- Be serious and discipline yourselves (1 Pet 4:7).
- Be hospitable (1 Pet 4:9).
- Outdo each other in showing honor (Rom 12:10).
- Maintain constant love and serve each other with your gifts (1 Pet 4:8, 10).

---

51. Jesus was speaking about how the washing of hands does not make one clean, but it is the state of one's heart that makes one acceptable to God. In other words, what does your heart have to offer people? Kindness? Gentleness? Patience? Remember, our hearts also contain the healing power of the Holy Spirit and the knowledge of Christ. So, even if we have no money, *every* Christian still has something good to give.

Every work Jesus did stemmed from love, whether it was healing, forgiving, feeding, teaching, visiting, defending, befriending, or praying. Therefore, whatever works we choose to do as we go about living life, should also stem from love: if we speak, we should speak in love; if we serve, we must serve with love; if we give, let us give to others with love; if we teach, then we teach with love; if we correct, we must be sure to correct with love. If we do anything without the sacrifice of love, then we have done the deed in vain and have wrongly represented God on earth. Love is both patience and kindness. Love is not envious of others, or boastful, or arrogant, or rude to others. Love supports and encourages. Love never expects or demands its own way because love is submissive. Love is not irritable or easily angered and it does not grow resentful. Love is not partial. Love does not rejoice in wrong. Instead, it rejoices in truth. Love suffers. Love believes. Love hopes. Love honors. Love respects. Love sees and treats their neighbor as themselves. This is how Jesus worked. This is how we must learn to work, slowly and one day at a time, depending upon the Holy Spirit to teach us about all these perfect attributes.

> By this everyone will know that you are my disciples, if
> you have love for one another. —Jn 13:35

4. "Abstains from works of darkness."
Abstaining from works of darkness is just as important as setting our minds to doing good works. This is because the

works of the flesh counteract our works of faith.

> Live by the Spirit, I say, and do not gratify the desires of the flesh. For what the flesh desires is opposed to the Spirit, and what the Spirit desires is opposed to the flesh; for these are opposed to each other, to prevent you from doing what you want. But if you are led by the Spirit, you are not subject to the law. Now the works of the flesh are obvious: fornication, impurity, licentiousness, idolatry, sorcery, enmities, strife, jealousy, anger, quarrels, dissensions, factions, envy, drunkenness, carousing, and things like these.
> —*Gal 5:16-21*

> But let none of you suffer as a murderer, a thief, a criminal, or even as a mischief maker. —*1 Pet 4:15*

We may not like to contemplate the fact that the way we live our private lives has any relevance at all upon our faith in Jesus, but it does. Sin damages the testimony of Jesus because it is deceitful to bear witness to one thing, all while our (unloving) actions or words refute that same belief. It is damaging to say, "Jesus is alive and sees all" while hidden personal sin says, "Nobody can see me." It is just as difficult to say, "I am a disciple of Jesus" if inaction, lack of knowledge, self-indulgence, harsh judgments, and lack of love *completely overshadows* that statement.[52]

We really are to lay aside our own self-seeking desires in the hope of attaining something far greater—a new life lived in the love of God, set upon the indestructible foundation of Jesus. We are to lose our lives here in order to gain them with God.

స్తో ఆ

I know your works—your love, faith, service, and patient endurance. I know that your last works are greater than the first. —*Revelation 2:19*

* For a review of this chapter and to answer reflective questions, see the companion guide: *Preparing ... The Testimony.*

52. The Holy Spirit is working in each of us to teach us how to love; this is a life-long process with many mistakes made along the way. God is gracious and patient, as a loving parent is with a child; God doesn't get tired of helping us to grow in love.

CHAPTER SEVEN

Generational Faith:
Passing on Your Testimony

Train children in the right way, and when old,
they will not stray.

—Proverbs 22:6

Every Christian can give powerful testimony to Jesus. Tragedy, heartbreak, and overcoming obstacles are not prerequisites; however, knowing who Jesus is, is a prerequisite. As I said in the last chapter, the strongest testimonies come from people who both grow in the knowledge of Christ and live in active faith, all while directed by love. Therefore, long-time Christians, those Christians who were introduced to Christ at a young age and were raised in a Christian family, should be the ones to have the strongest testimonies. After all, they have had the most opportunity to read the Bible and learn about Jesus; they have had the most opportunity to step out in faith and do good works; they have had the most opportunity to pray (and be prayed for) and be directed by God. Also, many have had Christian parents who were able to teach them and

102

inspire them to follow Jesus and the Holy Spirit. Ultimately, long-time Christians have had more time (as well as more support) to be taught how to love like Jesus and become active in spiritual things.

Sadly though, for many long-time Christians, growth is not happening as it should, and often faith in Jesus fades away altogether. After all, how many times have we heard, or perhaps stated ourselves, "I went to church all my life and I never understood what it all meant or why we were even going." *How is it that our Christian faith, through the generations, tends to become stale and then suddenly irrelevant?* The answer is found in the Old Testament:

> Moreover, that whole generation was gathered to their ancestors, and another generation grew up after them, who did not know the LORD or the work that he had done for Israel. *—Judg 2:10*

The book of Judges portrays a group of people continually forgetting their spiritual heritage. Every time the Israelites forgot about their God, what He had promised and what He had done, they withdrew from Him. After they withdrew, they eventually began worshiping idols, which in turn disappointed God because then they had not only forgotten about Him, but had also replaced Him with something utterly useless. God, in turn, then allowed His wayward, forgetful children to be punished by other nations. Thereby encouraging them to cry out for help, and God would once again gather them close. Through this process, the Israelites learned to worship *YHWH* all over again.

We're not much different from those early Israelites, sometimes forgetting not just the truths of our faith, but also the experiences behind our faith. Not surprisingly then, both truth and experience—our personal testimony—must be passed down to our children as a foundation for their faith to grow on. However, the way we testify to our children differs radically from the way the Israelites testified to their children.

Old Covenant vs. New Covenant

It was because of the Israelites' rather intense aptitude for forgetting God's commandments as well as the miracles He had done, that the following Proverb was written:

> Train children in the right way,[53]
> and when old, they will not stray. —*Prov 22:6*

The Old Testament context of this proverb is God's covenant. This is because in the Old Testament there are only two paths from which a child could choose: "the way of righteousness" and "the path of the fool." The first path consisted of following God's covenant commandments and His teachings; this is the path Israelite parents desperately wanted their children to follow and stay on. Succeeding on this path, as you can imagine, required dedicated discipline:

---

53. "In the right way" is literally, "upon the mouth of his way." "Upon the mouth of" is a Hebrew idiom meaning, "according to" or "in accord with." A servant would respond to a master, "upon the mouth of" or "at the command of" his superior.

My child, keep your father's commandment,
and do not forsake your mother's teaching.[54]
Bind them upon your heart always;
tie them around your neck.
When you walk, they will lead you;
when you lie down, they will watch over you;
and when you awake, they will talk with you.
For the commandment is a lamp and the teaching a
light,
and the reproofs of discipline are the way of life.
—Prov 6:20-23

The second path spoken about in the book of Proverbs is "the path of the fool." Following this path was somewhat less difficult. After all, to succeed on this path an Israelite merely needed to follow his own evil and foolish desires, ignoring the commandments of God:

The wise of heart will heed commandments,
but a babbling fool will come to ruin. *—Prov 10:8*

Fools think their own way is right,
but the wise listen to advice. *—Prov 12:15*

Fools mock at the guilt offering,
but the upright enjoy God's favor. *—Prov 14:9*

---

54. It was up to both parents to train children to follow *YHWH*. See also 2 Tim 1:5.

Since God's Old Covenant was not meant for just one generation of Israelites, but was intended for *all* the following generations, this required the Israelites to train their children to choose the path of righteousness and *stay* on the path of righteousness:

He [God] established a decree in Jacob,
and appointed a law in Israel,
which he commanded our ancestors
to teach to their children. —*Ps 78:5*

Teach them [the commandments] to your children, talking about them when you are at home and when you are away, when you lie down and when you rise.
—*Deut 11:19*

If parents could manage to train their children to stay in covenant relationship with God—by obeying the Ten Commandments—all would go well for their children: the God of Creation would be their God and they would be His special people. *But* if their children eventually forgot about God and went down another path (the path of the fool), following after other gods, then the worst would happen, and it did happen. The same is true for us. We must also stay on the right path. Except now, we are to stay on the path of righteousness *in the New Covenant*:

But now we are discharged from the law, dead to that which held us captive, so that we are slaves not under

the old written code but in the new life of the Spirit.
—*Rom 7:6*

Our competence is from God, who has made us competent to be ministers of a new covenant, not of letter but of spirit; for the letter kills, but the Spirit gives life. —*2 Cor 3:5-6*

Now if the ministry of death, chiseled in letters on stone tablets, came in glory so that the people of Israel could not gaze at Moses' face because of the glory of his face, a glory now set aside, how much more will the ministry of the Spirit come in glory? —*2 Cor 3:7-8*

This may sound absolutely crazy, but the unfortunate truth is many Christian parents (and church pastors) are training Christian children (and parishioners) to follow the path of death—that being the Old Testament form of righteousness: love God and obey the Ten Commandments. This, of course, doesn't sound like such a terrible deed. After all, loving God is good and obeying the Ten Commandments is good. But—and here's the scary part—following the path of Old Testament righteousness ultimately leads to death. The apostle Paul called it the "ministry of death." Loving God and obeying the Ten Commandments may sound spiritual and following them might lead to good decision making, but they are not spiritual. And they are not for Christians. They are merely a shadow of something—no, of *someone* divine:

> Since the law has only a shadow of the good things
> to come and not the true form of these realities, it
> can never, by the same sacrifices that are continually
> offered year after year, make perfect those who
> approach. —*Heb 10:1*

It is the Holy Spirit who works at perfecting us, not the Ten Commandments. We, those who have been baptized into the *New Covenant*, are to train our children in accordance with the *Ministry of the Spirit*. Merely teaching our children to love God is no longer enough simply because God has now revealed His Son and His Spirit. Our love must now encompass the whole of God. Similarly, just obeying the Ten Commandments (and the teachings of the Old Testament) is no longer sufficient because now God has revealed the *spiritual commandments*. Jesus is the one who lived according to the ministry of the Spirit. The spiritual commandments Jesus taught his apostles and disciples are not necessarily different from the Ten Commandments, but they do strike much, much deeper:

> You have heard that it was said to those of ancient
> times, "You shall not murder"; and "whoever murders
> shall be liable to judgment." But I say to you that if you
> are angry with a brother or sister, you will be liable to
> judgment; and if you insult a brother or sister, you will
> be liable to the council; and if you say, "You fool," you
> will be liable to the hell of fire. —*Mt 5:21-22*[55]

---

55. Read Mt 5:17-48 for Jesus' teaching on the commandments.

Under the New Covenant, God is concerned not just with our actions, but rather with our hearts. In other words, unlike the Ten Commandments that could only judge our *outer* actions (such as "do not murder," "do not steal," and "do not worship idols"), the Holy Spirit is capable of judging our hearts ("do not hold anger in your heart"). Therefore, the Old Testament and the New Testament—though similar—are very much different. The difference is: the New Testament is deeply, deeply ... *personal.*

If we merely teach our children to love God and obey the Ten Commandments, eventually their Christian faith will die, maybe not in the first generation but eventually it will die. The Bible guarantees it. However, following the Spirit of life leads to life. And parents (and pastors) who learn to walk in the Spirit, teach in the Spirit, worship in the Spirit, and train in the Spirit will accomplish an amazing work. We are not here to obey the Ten Commandments. We are here to obey the Holy Spirit—the law of the ministry of love, God who dwells within us. Again, Romans 13:10 tells us, "Love does no wrong to a neighbor; therefore, love is the fulfilling of the law."

However, despite our being under a New Covenant, the Spirit will uphold the old law. The Spirit will not change any word God has spoken. The word of God stands, but it stands in a *deeper* and *spiritual* fashion. Deeper meaning, it reaches to the core of our being; and spiritual meaning, it does not just exist here in the natural, but the ministry of love extends into eternity.[56]

Our children must get to know the New Covenant in order to survive and thrive in Christianity. And trust me, once someone has met the Spirit of life it is a hard task to walk away from such an amazing person. But here lies the problem: few of us have any real experience in dealing with the Spirit, so we turn to what we do know: God and the Ten Commandments. So how do we straighten ourselves out if we have been inadvertently following the Old Covenant? Teaching and testifying is key.[57]

Training Our Children Through Teaching and Testifying

It has been said that in three generations a family's faith can die. Personally, I like to believe it doesn't die at all—it just decreases and then lies dormant. (Until the Spirit has the inclination to stir it up again!) But still, the saying has merit. Just three short generations and faith diminishes: the first spirit-filled victim falls prey to complacency, tradition then steals away the second, and the third generation? They get swallowed up by forgetfulness. Suddenly, there hangs a confused family portrait that doesn't know why their grandmother ever went to church in the first place.

---

56. Many people get confused regarding how the Sabbath law relates to the New Testament. For further study see the appendix: "A Short Description of The Sabbath Rest" at the end of this book.

57. We still must study the Old Testament because the Old Testament is the history of our faith as well as prophecy. It teaches us about the New Testament and God's plan in general; whereas, living by the Old Testament is the ministry of death.

Take me for instance. I am a first generation believer. Neither my mother nor my father, even though they had been raised around Christian beliefs themselves, purposefully raised me to believe in Jesus. Religious discussion was definitely not part of our family life. And although my mother sent me to Catholic school, Sunday school, and even Mass a few times, she never taught me what any of it meant. I suppose this is because she didn't know what it all meant herself. Also, my grandparents, if they knew about Jesus, didn't tell me about him. However, I knew they were Catholic because of the cross and the picture of the Last Supper on their wall. Often times, I wanted to ask them about their spiritual beliefs—to have things explained to me, to hear why this cross and this picture were important—but I thought that would be silly. After all, I felt like I was supposed to *somehow* already know these things. I didn't want to seem stupid. In matters of religion, I stayed silent and … frustrated. That is until I turned sixteen, and I met a man and a woman who took the time to take me under their wings in order to teach me about the New Age. Finally, I had someone willing to teach me about spiritual things. After this, whatever I knew about Christianity began to be replaced by more (seemingly) interesting things.

For whatever reason, for many Christian families "religious talk" sometimes falls into the category of "sex" or "politics." Maybe this happens because we feel uncomfortable talking about something we know little about, or maybe we're just afraid of messing up an important spiritual conversation, oftentimes turning to prayer instead (which is also important). Or, maybe we're not that interested in the subject in the first place. I don't know. What I do know is it is extremely important to realize that whatever information we have regarding Father, Spirit, and Son should be passed down—in a gentle and enjoyable way—as a spiritual inheritance.

This doesn't mean we merely pass down religious practices. It means we *talk*. We talk about *why* we believe Jesus is alive and *how* we came to know him, adding in what we have *seen and heard* and *done* along our Christian journey. Perhaps adding to the mix what our parents and grandparents (and even our friends) saw and heard regarding Jesus and the Spirit. We can testify to our children about how *exactly* faith in Jesus overcomes the world. We can tell stories, give personal examples, show our children how to walk in faith, and teach them what the Bible reveals. We must share with our children what we know about Jesus—even if we know little. Ultimately, teaching our children to hunger and thirst after Christ and his Spirit is what we need to do if we want the next generation to desire this new life. If we do not teach our children to stay in New Covenant relationship, we will fall prey to the same trap that caught the Israelites—complacency and forgetfulness:

> They [The Christians] did not keep God's [New] covenant, but refused to walk according to his ~~law~~ [Spirit]. They forgot what he [Jesus] had done, and the miracles that he had shown them.
> —*Ps 78:10-11 (insertions and deletions, mine)*

Training Our Children Through Action

Perhaps just as damaging as not explaining and sharing our New Testament faith with our children is failing to put our faith into action. Inaction, or action that is contrary to our set of Christian beliefs, can undermine our children's faith. I cannot tell you how many times I've had to apologize to my children for acting or speaking out of anger. Children aren't dumb. They can smell a rotten deal from a mile away. If I am preaching a gospel that walks according to the Spirit of Christ, the Spirit of love, patience, and self-control, and I don't perform in a loving way, then my children may start to consider me a fraud. Eventually, they may even start to consider Jesus a fraud.

Ultimately, a Christian faith based on anything else besides faith and love (rules, judgment, or even tradition) is easily dismissed once a child leaves home. As James taught:

> But be doers of the word, and not merely hearers who deceive themselves. —*Jas 1:22*

When it comes to passing down faith in the Trinity of God (Father, Spirit, and Son) to our children, symbolic icons such as a dove or a cross firmly planted on our wall won't achieve deep faith. Observing religious holidays won't accomplish it either. Having children attend church won't guarantee a rock-solid foundation. Sending our kids to a Christian school won't always deliver. Mark Holmen, in his book *Faith Begins at Home,* describes his surprise when as a youth pastor he was asked to participate in a "Most Significant Religious

Influences" survey. He was surprised because the number one influencer in a Christian youth's life was "mom" and number two was "dad" (youth group leader ranked thirteenth).[58] Quite frankly, this shouldn't surprise us. After all, biblically, the primary teachers for children have always been parents. The book of Proverbs tells us:

> Hear, my child, your father's instruction,
> and do not reject your mother's teaching;
> for they are a fair garland for your head,
> and pendants for your neck. —*Prov 1:8-9*

Of course, knowing this means we cannot expect our church or our school to be the primary educators of our children in matters of faith. Our faith must be passed down to our children in a personal, meaningful, fully engaged, New Testament way. Even after doing so, eventually, our children must experience Christ and the Spirit for themselves. After all, just like the woman at the well who gave testimony to those in her city, everyone must experience Jesus for themselves:

> They said to the woman, "It is no longer because of what you said that we believe, for we have heard for ourselves, and we know that this is truly the Savior of the world." —*Jn 4:42*

---

58. See Holmen, *Faith Begins at Home*, 43.

Our Spiritual History

The Israelites were trained to live by testimony. Generation after generation the stories were told: God brought us out of Egypt, miracles were done, angels were seen, a savior was promised. We can learn to do the same within our own Christian families. For instance, DJ and I have three children. They will be raised as Christians. They will not have the sort of "coming to Jesus" testimony that I have. After all, I had to fight to come to Jesus, the darkness wanted to keep me. My three daughters will now benefit from my and DJ's beliefs and actions—as long as we continue to testify to them and teach them. And as we keep our spiritual history alive, our children will be more prone to want to step into it and keep it going.

Like the Israelites, DJ and I must learn to tell our children our stories: "a savior was promised, his name is Jesus; he did a miracle for your mommy and his Spirit spoke to your daddy." Let's not allow the busyness of life to keep us from speaking with our children about issues of faith. Let's talk with them as we drive to soccer and as we pray with them at night.

My children love to hear faith stories. My oldest daughter, Deanna, likes to be told the story of when she saw an angel. She was only four years old at the time. Today, I doubt if she can actually remember the event at all, but she knows how the story goes because we go over it again and again.

One evening in winter, while DJ and I were arguing over how to properly stack the dishes into the dishwasher, Deanna suddenly whispered, "Oh no, I see ... I see *shadow monsters*."

Surprised and worried by her eerie tone of voice, we turned. Deanna was standing on top of a kitchen chair, peering out the kitchen window into the dark night. We inched closer to listen, and as we did she murmured once again, "I see shadow monsters and they're fighting angels." Here Deanna stopped, then with a quick jolt of energy she continued, "Oh! But the angels are winning!" After uttering that last statement, she hopped off her chair and bounded into the living room to play, fully convinced the angels had everything under control.[59]

Through hearing this story over and over again, and by teaching Deanna that our trust (despite shadow monsters lurking outside) is in Jesus, the leader of God's army (Rev 19:14) who sends angels to help people (Heb 1:14), when Deanna grows older and begins to read the Bible herself, this event will be secured in her mind and the Bible won't seem so implausible to her. She will remember the night when she saw angels.

Similarly, I once decided to try to teach my middle daughter, Darby, that praying to God is important and that we can trust God to help us. In all sincerity, I just wanted Darby to know God hears her prayers. I wanted prayer to be part of her life from early on. I had no idea God was going to outright prove to her that He hears prayers.

One night as Darby lay in her bed, crying in a puddle of sweat because of a horrible nightmare, she cried out to God asking Him to send her mommy in to her. Next to her

---

59. Later, Deanna saw another angel who blew a trumpet. She told me the angel was, "big and shiny!"

bedroom, I lay asleep in my bed. Suddenly I heard a voice yell at me in my dream: "Get up!" I immediately awoke and asked, "What is it God?" That's when I heard Darby crying. Upon going in to her I said, "God woke me up, Darby. What's going on?"

"I asked God to wake you up," she whimpered. "I needed help."

Darby now understands just how much God loves her. And now, as she reads her Bible, and as I teach her about Jesus and the Holy Spirit, she will understand that turning to her heavenly family is where true help comes from.

I have come to realize that God wants our children to have a strong Christian faith, and He is willing to help us out in this area. Of course, eventually our children will have to stand on their own, making their own decisions regarding what they want to believe and how they want to act, but our job as parents is to give them the best possible chance to grow in the right, and overwhelmingly, good direction.

* For a review of this chapter and to answer reflective questions, see the companion guide: *Preparing ... The Testimony*.

CHAPTER EIGHT

One Final Thought on Testimony: *Death*

> And they have overcome (conquered) him by means of the
> blood of the Lamb and by the utterance of their testimony,
> for they did not love and cling to life even when faced
> with death [holding their lives cheap till they had to die
> for their witnessing].
>
> —Revelation 12:11, Amplified Bible

I have a wonderful mentor by the name of Pastor Gary. We often gab about Bible history, the demise of the prophet Balaam,[60] and, well ... *death*. (He's always sure he's going to die tomorrow, and I suppose one day he'll be right.) I, myself, am not one for having death continually on my mind, but lately it has been. Death has been on my mind simply because death is linked with testimony. After all, when a testimony becomes a whole life, like that of the early disciples and apostles, that very life suddenly becomes a serious threat to the enemy. It shouldn't come as a surprise then that the

---

60. Balaam, although a prophet, "loved the wages of doing wrong." See 2 Pet 2:15.

Greek word for "testimony" (*marturiŏn*) is the source for our word "martyr." Either way you look at it, whether dying for the gospel is a good thing or a depressingly nasty thing, it would be impossible to say the subject of biblical testimony had been completely covered without bringing up this rather macabre subject.

A list of the disciples killed or hurt for giving clear, bold, effective testimony, both in speech and works, is rather startling. First John the Baptist is beheaded. Stephen is then stoned to death. James dies by the sword, and Paul and Silas are flogged and put in Jail.[61] The apostle John is imprisoned on Patmos.[62] Jesus' brother James is stoned and clubbed to death. Paul is eventually beheaded, and Peter is crucified.[63] It was Jesus who warned his disciples they would be treated in this way:

> Brother will betray brother to death, and a father his child, and children will rise against parents and have them put to death; and you will be hated by all because of my name. But the one who endures to the end will be saved. —Mt 10:21-22

And it is the book of Revelation that confirms this link:

> Then I saw thrones, and those seated on them were given authority to judge. I also saw the souls of those

---

61. See Mt 14:10; Acts 7:59; 12:2; 16:19-23.

62. See Rev 1:9.

63. See Maier, *Eusebius*, 71-75 for a description of James', Paul's, and Peter's death.

who had been beheaded for their testimony to Jesus
and for the word of God. —*Rev 20:4*

When he opened the fifth seal, I saw under the altar
the souls of those who had been slaughtered for the
word of God and for the testimony they had given;
they cried out with a loud voice, "Sovereign Lord, holy
and true, how long will it be before you judge and
avenge our blood on the inhabitants of the earth?"
—*Rev 6:9-10*

The reason for the uncomfortable pairing of testimony
and death is because of spiritual warfare. Ultimately, the fight
between good and evil takes place in the realm of testimony.
After all, Satan does not want Jesus revealed. Every person
who becomes enlightened to the spiritual nature and person
of Jesus, becoming fruitful in knowledge *and* good deeds,
destabilizes his evil influence and instead enlarges Jesus'
kingdom on earth.[64] The truth is, as our Christian testimonies
grow stronger so will the spiritual warfare against us.

Because testimony about Jesus and death often go hand-
in-hand, giving testimony is not for the unprepared. If you
plan on giving testimony about Jesus be aware: Satan desires
to void your testimony by any means he can. Here in North
America we may not have to fear decapitation or being
thrown into jail, but physical death is not the only way to
destroy a testimony. Falling into embarrassing, hurtful, or

---

64. Reminiscent of "Do not be overcome by evil, but overcome evil
with good" (Rom 12:21).

disrespectful situations because of lust, greed, envy, or hate does just as good of a job. We should remember, if we slander (blaspheme) Christ with our words and/or our actions then, unfortunately, we should expect Satan to seek benefit from it:

> While you preach against stealing, do you steal? You that forbid adultery, do you commit adultery? You that abhor idols, do you rob temples? You that boast in the law, do you dishonor God by breaking the law? For, as it is written, "The name of God is blasphemed among the Gentiles because of you." —*Rom 2:21-24*

Satan wants us to mess up so he can attempt to destroy our influence on earth.[65] But Jesus, knowing we *will* mess up, disciplines us so we may continue on with him. Through this process we learn to be holy through suffering:

> But if we [Christians] judged ourselves, we would not be judged. But when we are judged by the Lord, we are disciplined so that we may not be condemned along with the world. —*1 Cor 11:31-32*

> My child, do not regard lightly the discipline of the Lord, or lose heart when you are punished by him; for the Lord disciplines those whom he loves, and chastises every child whom he accepts. Endure trials for the sake of discipline. God is treating you as children; for

---

65. Sometimes people testify wrongly about us, and our testimony is damaged because of lies and rumors mixed with misunderstood truth. See Lk 23:2 for an example using Jesus.

what child is there whom a parent does not discipline?
—*Heb 12:5-7*

I [Paul] do not even judge myself. I am not aware
of anything against myself, but I am not thereby
acquitted. It is the Lord who judges me. —*1 Cor 4:3-4*

However, if we do happen to suffer—specifically for
trusting in Jesus—we are not to feel shame:

Yet if any of you suffers as a Christian, do not consider
it a disgrace, but glorify God because you bear this
name. —*1 Pet 4:16*

If you see yourself as a testimonial evangelist, a person
whose main passion is speaking about Jesus through whatever
means God has gifted you, then be sober about your mission.
Be ready for the trials ahead. Scripture tells us to become
dead to the world (Gal 6:14). Becoming dead to the world
helps ensure our safety so our misguided desires cannot tempt
us and Satan cannot be allowed to destroy our testimony.
When we do mess up, as we will from time to time, suffering
through discipline with complete repentance is always our
best option. Eventually, we will learn to die to ourselves and
to the world in order to become holy to God:

You want something and do not have it; so you commit
murder. And you covet something and cannot obtain
it; so you engage in disputes and conflicts. You do not
have, because you do not ask. You ask and do not

receive, because you ask wrongly, in order to spend what you get on your pleasures. Adulterers! Do you not know that friendship with the world is enmity with God? Therefore whoever wishes to be a friend of the world becomes an enemy of God. —*Jas 4:2-4*

Spiritual warfare is not a glamorous fight where we continually blast demons from our presence. Rather, it is a lifestyle of drawing closer to Jesus and the Holy Spirit, seeking them, becoming like them, by both embracing and suffering through discipline, while at the same time testifying boldly to the truth of who Jesus is, even as we examine our own hearts in order to abstain from vain works of darkness. It is a life of self-sacrifice, servant-leadership, learning, prayer, unity, discipline, peace with believers, sober thinking, and love. It is a lifestyle of Christ-righteousness. It is not conformity to Christian-culture rules. Rather, it is an illumination of our individual, beautiful personalities and a conforming of our nature, character, and works to the holy, yet compassionate, Jesus. It is not a set pattern of rules or a hand-me-down religion. It is experiencing God's Christ and God's Spirit and seeking the will of God. It is a life of communing with the Spirit of God, allowing the Spirit to teach us while the Spirit whittles away at our fleshy nature, slowly restoring a perfect spiritual one. And it is not easy.

The Bible is not the "rule book for life." It is an invitation to journey into a radically new kind of life, a life where both our deeds and words testify about Jesus through the ministry of the Holy Spirit: love.

When all is said and done in this life, I want to be at peace with three things: that I wasn't ashamed of the gospel of Christ that saved me, that I suffered through discipline with repentance and patience, and that I grew in my portrayal of Jesus here on earth by developing in faith and love. I want desperately to be part of the vision Ezra saw:

> I, Ezra, saw on Mount Zion a great multitude that I could not number, and they all were praising the Lord [YHWH] with songs. In their midst was a young man of great stature, taller than any of the others, and on the head of each of them he placed a crown, but he was more exalted than they. And I was held spellbound. Then I asked an angel, "Who are these, my lord?" He answered and said to me, "These are they who have put off mortal clothing and have put on the immortal, and have confessed the name of God. Now they are being crowned, and receive palms." Then I said to the angel, "Who is that young man who is placing crowns on them and putting palms in their hands?" He answered and said to me, "He is the Son of God, whom they confessed in the world." So I began to praise those who had stood valiantly for the name of the Lord. Then the angel said to me, "Go, tell my people how great and how many are the wonders of the Lord God that you have seen."
> —2 Esd 2:42-48, NRSV with Apocrypha

One Final Thought on Testimony: *Death*

* For a review of this chapter and to answer reflective questions, see the companion guide: *Preparing ... The Testimony*.

INTRODUCTION TO BOOK THREE

Preparing ... The Testimony

But they have conquered him by the blood of the Lamb and by
the word of their testimony, for they did not cling to life even
in the face of death.

—Revelation 12:11

This companion guide is not
your typical Bible study. It is not
a simple guide meant to help
you prepare a story about how
you came to believe in Christ.
This book goes even further. It
will help you discover, examine,
understand, and value your
own personal faith. As well, the
chapter by chapter overview
and discussion questions will
help readers to focus on key aspects of both *Studying ... The
Testimony* and *Living ... The Testimony*, so that the material can
be thoroughly understood and discussed.

Introduction to Book Three

Whatever state of growth your faith is currently in be encouraged, because it is your faith ... it is invaluable, precious, and it has the ability to destroy the enemy.

Preparing ... The Testimony:
A Companion Guide For Individual or Group Study

* This book includes numerous questions meant to guide readers as they write their own personal testimony.

৵ ৶

Purchase this title at www.deidrehavrelock.com

A Short Description of The Sabbath Rest: *Warning! It May Not Be What You Think!*

I found myself, one evening, sitting around a table with about twelve women. We were all volunteering with a women's ministry, and this was the yearly potluck get together where we bonded and celebrated the past year. As I was enjoying a lovely curry dish, someone blurted out, "So what about that Sabbath?! Are we supposed to rest or not?" Well, what ensued was a series of *ummms,* followed by a few rambling statements about not following the Old Testament. The uncomfortable truth was, we didn't totally understand how the Sabbath rest related to the New Covenant. I remember thinking, this is important. We should know this.

To Rest, Or Not To Rest

Under the Old Testament law the Israelites were taught to keep the Sabbath, resting once every week: "Six days you shall labor and do all your work. But the seventh day is a sabbath to the LORD your God; you shall not do any work" (Ex 20:9-10). But under the New Testament we are told, "We are discharged from the law, dead to that which held us captive, so that we are slaves not under the old written code but in the new life of the Spirit" (Rom 7:6). *Does this mean we should not partake in the Sabbath rest?* And if we are not to obey the Sabbath law, why do the scriptures say: "Do we then overthrow the law by this faith? By no means! On the contrary, we uphold the law" (Rom 3:31)? *How are we to understand the Sabbath rest in light of the New Testament?* Do we rest? And if we're supposed to be resting, why does going to church sometimes feel like such work?! The answer is found in the four verses below:

1. "For when there is a change in the priesthood, there is necessarily a change in the law as well" (Heb 7:12).
2. "But it is not the spiritual that is first, but the physical, and then the spiritual" (1 Cor 15:46).
3. "For we know that the law is spiritual; but I am of the flesh, sold into slavery under sin" (Rom 7:14).
4. "For the law of the Spirit of life in Christ Jesus has set you free from the law of sin and of death" (Rom 8:2).

In order to understand the two laws (the spiritual law of life and the physical law of sin and death) being spoken about in the aforementioned verses, take a look at the lists below. They outline a few of the major differences:

Old (Physical) Law—The Written Law Of The Ten Commandments

- The priesthood that mediates this covenant and law is established through Moses and the tribe and *sons of Levi*.

Therefore, men work in this priesthood. Moses (the judge) and his brother Aaron (the high priest) are from the tribe of Levi.[66]

- This law judges outward actions based on witnesses' testimonies; the witnesses must literally view the sin.
- Judgment is delivered once the sin is made public and after testimony is given.
- This law is a written document of promise. It was originally written on stone. Therefore, this law is physical.
- The high priest in connection to this law *always dies*, and so a new high priest must be continually installed. Therefore, this is a *natural* priesthood.
- The Sabbath rest is a perpetual sign to the Israelites. It is meant to remind the people that it is God who *sanctifies* (cleanses) them.[67] People attached to this covenant must rest weekly. They must not prepare food or work at their jobs. If caught working and if convicted, the transgressor must be stoned to death.
- Worship and service of this law takes place in a man-made temple.
- Levite priests *work* in this temple on every Sabbath, assisting the high priest in order to minister to the people.

---

66. See Num 26:59. In order to be a high priest, one had to descend from the family of Aaron. See Num 3:10.

67. See Ex 31:12-13.

- This written covenant was broken.[68]

New (Spiritual) Law—The Holy Spirit Of Life

- The priesthood in connection to this law is established through the tribe of *Judah*. Jesus descends from Judah.
- Because a different tribe is chosen, a new law becomes active.
- This new law judges inward heart motivations which people cannot see, such as: "do not hold anger in your heart."[69]
- This law is written on the heart, through the indwelling of the Holy Spirit.[70] Therefore, this law is *spiritual*.
- God helps people connected to this law by "disciplining" them now, helping them to grow in love. Sometimes this discipline includes pressure, obstacles, and hardships.[71]
- Forgiveness is paramount in this law.[72]
- Final judgment by a court comes only when Jesus returns; he will then judge the hearts and deeds of all people.
- The new law is referred to as "the Ministry of the Spirit." Its main component is love:

---

68. See Isa 24:5: "For they have transgressed laws, violated the statutes, broken the everlasting covenant."

69. See Mt 5:22 for Jesus' teaching on this.

70. See Heb 8:10.

71. See 1 Cor 11:32: "But when we are judged by the Lord, we are disciplined so that we may not be condemned along with the world."

72. See Mt 6:15 "But if you do not forgive others, neither will your Father forgive your trespasses." Also, Mt 18:35.

> For you were called to freedom, brothers and sisters; only do not use your freedom as an opportunity for self-indulgence, but through love become slaves to one another. For the whole law is summed up in a single commandment, "You shall love your neighbor as yourself." If, however, you bite and devour one another, take care that you are not consumed by one another. Live by the Spirit, I say, and do not gratify the desires of the flesh. —*Gal 5:13-16*

- The new high priest who mediates this law is an eternal priest (he cannot die); therefore, this law is *eternal*.
- The priests in this priesthood are also eternal—both men and women have been chosen, cleansed, and have received new life.
- Priests work by offering a sacrifice of good deeds through faith and love.
- These priests work in temples that are their *bodies*.
- How does the Sabbath relate to this new law?

Putting it All Together

Under the Old Testament only male Levite priests, along with the high priest, were allowed to work on the Sabbath, in order to minister to the people:

> For the LORD your God has chosen Levi out of all your tribes, to stand and minister in the name of the LORD, him and his sons for all time. —*Deut 18:5*[73]

Through this Old Testament teaching, we understand that—while on duty in the temple—it was *improper* for a priest to rest on the natural Sabbath. In other words, if a priest was on duty, well ... then he was expected to work by preparing and offering sacrifices:

> Or have you not read in the law that on the sabbath the priests in the temple break the sabbath and yet are guiltless? —*Mt 12:5*

The New Covenant, like the Old Covenant, also has a priesthood. This new priesthood also has a high priest, and that high priest is Jesus:

> So also Christ did not glorify himself in becoming a high priest, but was appointed[74] by the one who said to him, "You are my Son, today I have begotten you"; as he says also in another place, "You are a priest

---

73. When people read "for all time" they often assume that the priesthood must still consist of "sons." But this first covenant was broken: "I took my staff Favor and broke it, **annulling** the covenant that I had made with all the peoples" (Zech 11:10, bold added).

74. Reminiscent of Num 18:7, "I give your priesthood as a gift."

forever, according to the order of Melchizedek."
—*Heb 5:5-6*[75]

Jesus' new priesthood, however, is far different from the old one. First of all, Jesus' priesthood is a *spiritual* priesthood, as opposed to a natural one. Therefore, this priesthood is *eternal*—it extends into the spiritual realm. In other words, Jesus and his priests have eternal life. Second, this high priest does not descend from the tribe of Levi, as dictated under the old law. Instead, Jesus descends from the tribe of Judah:

> Now if perfection had been attainable through the levitical priesthood—for the people received the law under this priesthood—what further need would there have been to speak of another priest arising according to the order of Melchizedek, rather than one according to the order of Aaron?[76] For when there is a change in the priesthood, there is necessarily a change in the law as well. Now the one of whom these things are spoken belonged to another tribe, from which no one has ever served at the altar. For it is evident that our Lord was descended from Judah, and in connection with that tribe Moses said nothing about priests.
> —*Heb 7:11-14*

---

75. Melchizedek, found in the Old Testament, was king of Salem meaning, "king of peace." He appeared offering bread and wine; see Gen 14:18. Jesus is also called the King of Peace; see Heb 7:2; Eph 2:14. Jesus also offered bread and wine; see Mt 26:26-28. Ps 110:4 predicts that another priest will come according to the order of Melchizedek.

76. Aaron was the first high priest; he was the brother of Moses.

Appendix

Also, this priesthood, unlike the old priesthood, worships and ministers not in a temple made with stones like the old temple built by King Solomon; instead, this priesthood worships and ministers in a temple made of "body united with Spirit":

> But you are a chosen race, a royal priesthood, a holy nation, God's own people, in order that you may proclaim the mighty acts of him who called you out of darkness into his marvelous light. —*1 Pet 2:9*

> Do you not know that you are God's temple and that God's Spirit dwells in you? If anyone destroys God's temple, God will destroy that person. For God's temple is holy, and you are that temple. —*1 Cor 3:16-17*

Since the presence of God dwells inside us—both men *and* women—filling us just like the presence of God once filled the temple made by Solomon, this means that—for us who are in the new covenant—Jesus' new priesthood is *always* in God's presence. Therefore, this priesthood is *always* on duty within the temple of their bodies. For example see the following:

1. Old Testament Temple Was Filled With The Spirit of God

> "Let your priests, O LORD God, be clothed with salvation. ..." When Solomon had ended his prayer,

fire came down from heaven and consumed the burnt offering and the sacrifices; and the glory of the LORD filled the temple. *—2 Chr 6:41, 7:1*

2. New Testament Temple(s) Are Filled With The Spirit of God

When the day of Pentecost had come, they [Jesus' disciples, both men and women] were all together in one place. And suddenly from heaven there came a sound like the rush of a violent wind, and it filled the entire house where they were sitting. Divided tongues, as of fire, appeared among them, and a tongue rested on each of them. All of them were filled with the Holy Spirit and began to speak in other languages, as the Spirit gave them ability. *—Acts 2:1-4*

Present your bodies as a living sacrifice, holy and acceptable to God, which is your spiritual worship. *—Rom 12:1*

Come to him, a living stone, though rejected by mortals yet chosen and precious in God's sight, and like living stones, let yourselves be built into a spiritual house, to be a holy priesthood, to offer spiritual sacrifices acceptable to God through Jesus Christ. *—1 Pet 2:4-5*

Because this new priesthood is eternal, they must wait for a true Sabbath rest. In other words, Jesus taught his disciples to *work as his priests* (by offering a sacrifice of good works) until he returns. As Jesus said, "Blessed is that slave whom his master will find at work when he arrives" (Mt 24:46).[77] Then, when Jesus returns—and all the work of Jesus' new priesthood is done—then, and only then, can a true, spiritual Sabbath rest be taken:

> For if Joshua had given them rest, God would not speak later about another day.[78] So then, a sabbath rest still remains for the people of God; for those who enter God's rest also cease from their labors as God did from his. Let us therefore make every effort to enter that rest, so that no one may fall through such disobedience as theirs.[79] —*Heb 4:8-11*

> And I heard a voice from heaven saying, "Write this: Blessed are the dead who from now on die in the

---

77. Just as the Levite priests were "attached" to Aaron in order to serve him, we belong to Christ. See Num 18:2, 4.

78. Joshua was leading the people into the Promised Land, which many understood to be God's place of promised rest. But since the Holy Spirit then later speaks (through King David) about another coming rest that we are to enter into, saying, "O that **today** you would listen to his voice! Do not harden your hearts …" (Ps 95:7-8, bold added), Joshua's rest cannot be the "the official Sabbath rest" that the Spirit was speaking about. David prophesied, long after Joshua, about another coming rest; therefore, there is a better rest coming for God's people. Read Heb 3 and 4 for more information on this topic.

79. Many Israelites did not make it to the Promised Land. They had unbelieving hearts and died in the desert. See Heb 3:19.

Lord." "Yes," says the Spirit, "they will rest from their labors, for their deeds follow them." —*Rev 14:13*

So the Sabbath rest remains, but it is a spiritual teaching and not merely an Old Testament law. The new priesthood now has a true rest coming to them, and our hearts eagerly await it. We understand that, for now, there is much work to do. Resting at this point is not an option. We must continue to overcome evil with good. Of course, this type of work is not about performing until our bodies wear out and we fall over, due to fatigue. Our work is more about "discipline and relationship": such as growing in the knowledge of Jesus, growing in character and in good deeds (any kind of good deed). Our work is about "building up each other through love."

Our coming rest will be a rest much like the one God took after completing creation: "Thus the heavens and the earth were finished, and all their multitude. And on the seventh day God finished the work that he had done, and he rested on the seventh day from all the work that he had done" (Gen 2:1-2). One day Jesus' new priesthood will be allowed to rest just as God rested.[80] We will rest because *all* the work of Christ's priesthood will be complete. There will be no more work to do, and rest will be welcomed. For now, however, we work.

---

80. The coming "Day" of rest may be the one-thousand-year reign of Christ; the time when Satan is bound in hell for a one-thousand-year period and peace reigns. Those people who have entered into God's spiritual Sabbath rest by the means of faith and love, will rule with Christ. This is the first resurrection. See Rev 20:2-6.

Appendix

ॐ ॐ

But Jesus answered them, "My Father is still working, and I also am working." For this reason the Jews were seeking all the more to kill him, because he was not only breaking the sabbath, but was also calling God his own Father, thereby making himself equal to God.

—*John 5:17-18*

BIBLIOGRAPHY

Holman, Mark. *Faith Begins at Home: the Family Makeover with Christ at the Center.* Ventura: Regal Books, 2005.

Maier, Paul L. (trans). *Eusebius: The Church History.* Grand Rapids: Kregel Publications, 1999.

Maier, Paul L. (trans). *Josephus: The Essential Works An Illustrated Condensation of Jewish Antiquities and The Jewish War.* Grand Rapids: Kregel Publications, 1988.

Robinson, George. *Essential Judaism: A Complete Guide to Beliefs, Customs, and Rituals.* New York: Simon and Schuster, Inc., 2000.

ABOUT THE AUTHOR

Deidre's goal as both a writer and a teacher is to introduce people to a deeply spiritual kind of Christianity while encouraging both men and women to *live the testimony with radical love.* In pursuit of this goal, Deidre teaches on numerous subjects including the importance of developing a clearly focused testimony. She often shares her own spiritual journey (which is included in book two of *The Testimony* series) so that others may experience Jesus through her life story.

Deidre's testimony is also available as both an ebook and paperback. It is a spiritual memoir told in two books. *Saving Mary: The Possession* is currently available; see <u>www.deidrehavrelock.com</u> for details.

We've all seen the horror of *The Exorcist*; we've experienced the drama of *Emily Rose*. We've watched heads spin, bodies contort, and we've seen holy water sprayed as young girls scream and thrash about. But what we haven't been offered is a candid account of possession from a first-person perspective. *What does the road to possession look like? What role does "faith" play in deliverance?* Travel with Deidre into the mysterious world of the supernatural. Awaken yourself to a world that isn't supposed to exist, a world that's as sinister as it is intriguing, and then emerge as a new person—invigorated, aware, and intent on living in the light.

Saving Mary:
Not Just Another Story About a Girl and Her Exorcist.

ౚ ಌ

Saving Mary: The Deliverance, coming soon.

ౚ ಌ

- Want to receive updates on new releases? Go to www.deidrehavrelock.com and Subscribe for Updates. I will never share your email with anyone else, and I will only email you regarding new releases.

- If you enjoyed this book, please take the time to leave a short review on Amazon. Your reviews are greatly appreciated!

THE TESTIMONY SERIES BY DEIDRE D HAVRELOCK

www.deidrehavrelock.com

Made in the USA
Charleston, SC
14 October 2013